Aloe Vera

A

Mission Discovered

Lee Ritter

Triputic

Dallas, TX

To Order:

1-800-331-1678

ISBN 0-9638609-0-9
First Printing 1993

DISCLAIMER

The Author does not intend to prescribe the use of Aloe vera in the treatment of any disease or ailment. The intent of this book is to make the reader aware of the information and testimonials available from third party sources.

The Author makes no recommendations in this book as to the the quality of any particular brand of Aloe vera.

ACKNOWLEDGMENTS

I am grateful to the many who have contributed to this book. To those who have shared their testimonies, listened to my message and responded, I express my deepest appreciation. To my office staff, thank you for your long efforts in gathering materials and reviewing the drafts.

There are two very special people who have contributed so great to the preparation of this book. Without the support of my wonderful wife who was always there with suggestions and support, I could never have written my story nor continued in my mission to bring the real truth about Aloe vera to so many. Donna Sylvester is a friend that I know God sent my way. She has located materials, carefully reviewed all the draft manuscripts, and made wonderful suggestions.

The author examing Aloe vera plant

CONTENT

CHAPTER 1

MY MISSION UNFOLDS

O World, thou chooseth not the better part!
It is not wisdom to be only wise,
And on the inward vision close the eyes,
But it is wisdom to believe the heart.
Columbus found a world, and had no chart,
Save one that faith deciphered in the skies;
To trust the soul's invincible surmise
Was all his science and his only art.
George Santayana[1]

At a very young age, I felt that God had a special mission for me. It was my vision, something I had to do to help others. My quest was to find that mission. At one time I considered the ministry. I set upon a great number of different paths, many of which didn't seem to lead anywhere—dead ends. But now, in retrospect, I see my journey like the pieces of a large jigsaw puzzle. The picture is at last complete enough that even though I cannot see all the details, my vision is clear. I know my mission is the advancement of Aloe vera, nature's miracle.

Now some of the pieces of the picture, which before made no sense, have purpose. My father died when I was a young boy. We never learned what caused his death. Everyone thought he looked healthy. The family just couldn't understand why he didn't feel well. He took a sudden change for the worse and died. He knew he was dying. None of us did. I couldn't understand why the doctor didn't treat him with a medicine that would cure him, and I was angry. Possibly that perplexity and anger gave direction to my quest.

Life was bad after my father died. I couldn't bear to watch my mother and new stepfather go without bare essentials for me. I remember my stepfather cutting pieces of cardboard and putting them in his shoes to cover the holes because he couldn't afford a pair of new ones. At the age of fourteen I left home alone, hitch-hiking from Wyoming to California with every-thing I owned. My suitcase was a paper sack. In the beginning I struggled just to survive. In California a lady let me sleep in her garage. I got a job working in a steel plant. From those struggles God gave me a deep empathy for the suffering and hardships of others, especially children. I have said so many times, "If in this life I can be responsible for adding one additional breath of life to a dying child or, in some small way, help to hold back just one tear of a saddened parent, relative or friend, life will have been worth it." And now, I have seen life-saving miracles occur.

But God has been good to me. He didn't say it would be easy and it hasn't been. I worked hard and with time I made my fortune, got my education, traveled this country many times and found a wonderful wife. Along the journey there were times when I even wondered if I had been wrong in believing I had a special mission. There were times when I struggled until my faith buried the creeping doubts. It took a long time for me to learn that the preparation must precede the mission and, with an eternity before Him, God doesn't conform to the demands of man's timetable.

Aloe vera first came to my attention and interest in the early 1980's. Through one of my businesses, I developed a close friendship with the western movie star, Dale Robertson. It began with our common interest in horses. He purchased Western equipment from one of my stores. Together we decided to develop a cosmetic line for men. We even hit upon a brand name which, in the sophistication of the 90's seems outrageously overt, *Clout*. Out of the beginnings of this venture came my first real contact with Aloe vera. We knew that the plant was purported to have positive medicinal value in topical applications. A large segment of the public knew this too. As a base for the cosmetics, Aloe was, we felt, a good marketing tool.

Dale lived in Oklahoma. He knew of a nearby cosmetic manufacturing company that used Aloe in its products. They seemed just right for manufacturing our product. But in the middle of negotiating an arrangement for private label manufacturing of our cosmetics, Dale's fortune took a turn for the worse. His Oklahoma bank went under, taking with it his deposits. Consequently Dale had to back out and the project never got off the ground.

I continued managing my other businesses and raising horses. Then one day I got a strange call. Doctor Terry Pulse, a physician in Texas, was having what appeared to be unbelievable success treating HIV positive patients with whole leaf Aloe vera juice. The caller thought that I might be interested. I was. Something felt right. I called Dr. Pulse. He told me that he had been conducting a study of 30 HIV positive patients (one non-compliant patient dropped out of the study, reducing the number to 29). Simplified considerably, the group of 29 broke down as follows: based on the modified Walter Reed Score (a method of determining from a set of factors the stage of AIDS development), fifteen had full blown AIDS. Twelve of the subjects met the criteria for AIDS Related Complex (ARC) and the remaining two were HIV seropositive, but asymptomatic. In other words, they were at three differently defined stages of the infection. The patients were put on a daily regimen of nutritional supplements and a minimum of 1200 milligrams of the active ingredients found in whole leaf Aloe vera juice.

After six months, 27 of the 28 patients had improved on their Walter Reed scores. All had improved on the Karnofsky Quality of Life Assessment Scores. There were substantial improvements in other medical tests indicating such things as an increase in the T-4 cell count, which reflects a boosting of the immune system and a drop in the P-24 core antigen activity.[2]

I remember asking Dr. Pulse what he had concluded from his study. He stated, "Aloe is to an AIDS patient such as insulin is to a diabetic." He further told me that his study clearly showed that Aloe vera played an active role in halting the progression of the AIDS virus.

I learned from Dr. Pulse that another study had been conducted by Dr. H. Reginald McDaniel, Chief of Pathology at Dallas-Fort Worth Medical Center. He had treated sixteen AIDS patients using 1,000 mg a day of orally administered Aloe. His study reflected that, after six months, six patients with advanced cases of AIDS showed a 20% improvement in symptoms while less seriously ill patients improved by an average of 71%. Dr. Pulse further confirmed that, like his tests, Dr. McDaniel's also reflected a drop in HIV antibody positive cell cultures. Also, symptoms such as fever, night sweats, diarrhea, and opportunistic infections were either eliminated or significantly reduced in all patients.

What I was hearing was astounding. At that time there were over 50,000 AIDS patients dying each year and the numbers were growing. The number has now more than doubled. I began to read everything I could locate on both Aloe vera and AIDS. I talked to everyone I could find who claimed any expertise with Aloe. There were studies or testimonials that indicated positive results when Aloe vera was used in the treatment of a variety of illnesses including: AIDS, tumors, cancer, a variety of dermatological conditions, ulcers, diabetes, gum diseases, hemorrhoids, heart disease, prostate infection, stomach ailments, and the list goes on.

Somewhere in my early reading I concluded that, if Aloe's curative contribution was even a fraction of what was indicated in the information I had come across, then this anhidrotic succulent, which looked like a cactus but came from the lily family, had to be truly nature's miracle plant. Later I made a video about some of the applications of the whole leaf Aloe vera concentrate in the treatment of AIDS, tumors and cancer. I titled the film, *Nature's Miracle*, and it has now been seen worldwide.

Once I had a good handle on the available
information about Aloe vera, I made a decision.
I awakened my wife, Susan, in the middle of the
night and said, "God has had a hand in my
involvement with Aloe vera. I am going to give
it all that I have. I ask you to support me. But
if you can't I certainly understand."

Susan replied, "Lee, if you really feel that
strongly about it, I'm with you all the way."
And she has been.

I decided on a plan. I would form a company,
Triputic, which would be both the finest source
of available information about Aloe vera and the
supplier of the best Aloe treatment products
available. Whatever it cost in time, money, and
other resources I would give. But I soon discovered that the Food and Drug Administration
(FDA) didn't have such altruistic motives. They
intervened, limiting Triputic to just an information source. In their bureaucratic, drug cartel-
lobbied eyes, if I shared research information
about the benefits of Aloe and then sold Aloe
vera products, I would be in violation of their
regulations because, by their standards, Aloe
vera had to be registered as a drug in order for

---

me to share information on its benefits. It is currently registered only as a food product. I'll cover the tragic interference of the FDA in another chapter.

Since I committed myself to sharing information about Aloe vera, I've become known internationally, presenting the story of whole leaf Aloe vera concentrate in some 39 foreign countries and in every state in the nation. Last week alone, we at Triputic had over 1700 telephone inquiries about Aloe. I've tested hundreds of Aloe products available on the market today. I've collected professional studies and gathered the testimonials of those who have witnessed the miraculous healing effects of Aloe. I've fought the Food and Drug Administration and other government regulatory agencies and I've taken on the frauds in the industry. This book is my story, the truth about Aloe vera.

CHAPTER 2

SEEING IS BELIEVING

Cynicism is intellectual dandyism.
George Meridith[3]

After Dr. Terry Pulse shared his research information and the results of treating AIDS patients with Aloe vera, I traveled to his clinic, interviewed the doctors, the staff, and AIDS patients and videotaped what was occurring. Two close friends, Wayne Osmond, of the famed performing Osmond Brothers, and Richard Callister, my attorney journeyed, with me. Wayne agreed to do the filming.

On the flight to Dallas, Texas, I further briefed my two friends about the studies of Dr. Pulse and Dr. McDaniel. My attorney was particularly cynical. How could some plant that grew best in hot, arid climates have the magic ability to improve AIDS patients and contribute to healing tumors, cancer, and a myriad of other diseases? If it were so magical, why weren't doctors using it and why hadn't they heard about it? Why hadn't the FDA approved it for treatment? They presented me with a flood of questions. Always the cynic, attorneys have questions and doubts. I patiently replied, "Wait and see."

I don't try to convince anyone. I never pre-scribe anything. I just share the facts that I have learned and the events that I have witnessed. First Dr. Pulse reviewed his study as we record-ed it on video. Then the patients arrived and one by one we taped their stories. Some wanted their likenesses masked because of their employ-ment or family. But all of them wanted other AIDS patients to know their miraculous story. These were patients who had previously been very sick with AIDS. They were confined to their beds, unable to work. They had the char-acteristic symptoms, including night sweats, nausea, and vomiting. They had been told by doctors that they were nearing the end and that nothing really could be done for them. The stories they told were astounding. They started on Dr. Pulse's regimen, drinking an Aloe bever-age throughout the day. With T-4 helper cell counts starting below 200 (frequently substantial-ly below) the counts had climbed to numbers like 400, 500, 800, and their symptoms had disappeared.

The final AIDS patient to be filmed was Michael Arrington. He was in the most serious condition of any of the patients, having been given 4 to 21 days to live. There had been 17 malignant tumors on his liver, with one the size of a baseball. We saw the X-rays and filmed them on our video, *Nature's Miracle*. His situation was terminal. The doctors had told him to go home and die. All this is documented on the *Nature's Miracle* video. There was no cure. Six months after starting on Aloe vera, the tumors were completely gone. There could be no disputing what Aloe vera had done. He had not been on other medicines.

Michael accompanied us across the street and down the block to the Dallas-Fort Worth Medical Center. Dr. H. Reginald McDaniel, Chief of Pathology at the hospital, showed us Michael's before and after X-rays. A very outspoken, blunt man, he shocked us by saying, "The use of Aloe vera will be the most important single step forward in the treatment of diseases in the history of mankind." I now sincerely believe that too.

Then Dr. McDaniel told us his story. It would

be an all too common story as I investigated in the months to come. Doctor McAnalley, Director of Research at Carrington Laboratories, had come into Dr. McDaniel's office and told him that five or six AIDS patients who were unable to get out of bed, go to school, or work drank aloe in large amounts and in a few weeks they began showing signs of improvement. Some were able to go back to work. Dr. McAnalley wanted Dr. McDaniel to do pathology lab studies for him on AIDS patients. McDaniel said that he considered it a cock and bull story and was not interested. However, he recounted that he had just returned from a trip and had viral pneumonia. He had failed three courses of antibiotics and was feeling very sick while talking to McAnalley. He made the comment to Doctor McAnalley, "I wouldn't give anything to anyone that I hadn't taken myself." Doctor McAnalley supplied bottles of Aloe vera for him, which he began to drink. Then he related,

> *...and in about two days I was much better. I didn't believe that what I was drinking was the cause because I thought it was about time I was getting well anyway. But the*

*thing that really impressed me was
that in about five days I no longer
was coughing up material out of my
lungs. They were perfectly clear
and this coughing syndrome usually
goes on for weeks with something
like this.*

From this experience Dr. McDaniel told us he
concluded he would do the pathology work that
would be required with the AIDS patients in the
study.

In addition to showing us the X-rays of Michael
Arrington's liver with the 17 malignant tumors
and the X-rays taken again six months later
showing only scar tissue, Dr. McDaniel showed
us X-rays of a lady who had breast cancer. She
drank Aloe vera and again X-rays confirmed the
disappearance of the cancer.

He further told us that with Green Monkey
cells, he was able to show that by adding ingredients from the Aloe plant, herpes virus and
measles virus proliferation were blocked in
direct correlation to the dose. He said that,
while it had taken them awhile to do it, they

finally co-cultured monocytes from human donors and were able to show inhibition of the AIDS virus in white cell cultures with the use of Aloe. There was increased survivability of the target cells that one would expect the virus to attack.

On the plane back to Utah, my attorney just shook his head and repeated several times, "Lee, if I hadn't seen it I wouldn't have believed it." My mission was beginning.

CHAPTER 3

ALOE VERA'S 4000 YEAR OLD HISTORY

Upon this point a page of history is worth a volume of logic.
New York Trust Co. v. Eisner[4]

The chief engineer for a large, international pharmaceutical company said to me recently, "Lee, we've known for some time about the benefits of Aloe vera but there's no incentive for us to put up the multi-millions it would cost to get it approved as a drug by the Federal Drug Administration." Estimated costs for obtaining FDA approval of a new drug can run from 100 to 300 million dollars.

I replied, "What do you mean no incentive? AIDS, cancer, tumors, ulcers, heart disease, burns, it's a miracle drug."

"You don't understand," he countered. "When we finish our research and obtain FDA approval and registration, there's nothing to patent. We would have no proprietary interest. Aloe vera is a natural drug protected from patent. Every drug company in the world would take advantage of our research and start producing Aloe drugs. The bottom line, profits aren't there."

What a condemnation of our society.

Medical healers of past civilizations, not having to deal with bureaucratic administrations, prescribed Aloe vera for a large variety of illnesses and ailments.

In about 1750 B.C. Sumerian clay tablets indicate the use of Aloe vera for medical purposes.[5] It appears that even earlier, perhaps as early as 4,000 B.C., drawings of it were found on temple walls in the tombs of the Pharaohs.[6] It is said that the Egyptians called it the Plant of Immortality.[7] It may have been one of the substances used in the embalming practice. The traditional use may have carried down to the time of Christ where we read of Aloe being applied to the body of Christ.

And they took the body of Jesus and wound it in linen clothes with the spices as the manner of the Jews is to bury.

John 19:39-40

Perhaps the Jews obtained their knowledge of the use of Aloe during the time they were in the land of Egypt.

There are five references in the Bible to Aloe.

As the valleys are they spread forth, as gardens by the river's side, as the trees of lign aloes which the Lord hath planted, [and] as cedar trees beside the waters.

Numbers 24:6

All thy garments [smell] of myrrh, and aloes, [and] cassia, out of the ivory palaces, whereby they have made thee glad.

Psalms 45:8

I have perfumed my bed with myrrh, aloes, and cinnamon.
Proverbs 7:17

Spikenard and saffron; calamus and cinnamon, with all trees of frankincense; myrrh and aloes, with all the chief spices:
Song of Solomon 4:14

And there came also Nicodemus, which at the first came to Jesus by night, and brought a mixture of Myrrh and aloes, about an hundred pound [weight].
John 19:39

By 1500 B.C., Aloe is mentioned in Egypt's *Papyrus Embers* where formulas containing Aloe are described for a variety of illnesses, both external and internal.[8]

By about 600 B.C. the use of Aloe appears in the Persian Empire, then throughout the Arab world and into India. The spread in its usage is undoubtedly attributable to Arab traders who plied their wares through much of the then civilized world.

Aloe vera, known as Ghee-guar-ka-palhtha in India,[9] is still used in that country for treating a variety of illnesses including ophthalmological disorders, enlargement of the spleen, hepatitis, skin disorders, musculoskeletal disorders, menstrual disorders, and as a purgative.[10]

In 1985, O.P. Agarwal, a medical doctor in India, presented to the American College of Angiology a paper reporting astounding results using Aloe vera in the treatment of 5,000 patients with atheromatous heart disease and diabetes.[11]

In the first century A.D., the Greeks were mentioning Aloe in their writings. Celsius saw its use as a purgative.[12] In his *Greek Herbal* Dioscorides indicated its use in the treatment of skin disorders such as boils, ulcerated genitals, dry itchy skin, bruises, hemorrhoids, tonsils, gums, mouth pain, and as an eye medicine.

> *Aloe....is of a strong scent, and*
> *very bitter to ye taster, but it is but*
> *of one root having a root as a*

stake. It grows in India very much, ...from when also ye extracted juice is brought. It also grows in Arabia and Asia and in certain sea-bordering places and Islands....It hath a power of binding, or procuring sleep, of drying, of thickening of bodies, and loosening of ye belly, and of cleansing of ye stomach being drank ye quantity of 2 spoonfuls with water cold, or warm milk;...it stops ye spitting of blood; and it cleanseth ye Icterus.

And it being swallowed also with Rosin, or taken either with water, or sod honey it looseth ye belly, but ye quantity of 3 drams doth fully purge. But being mixed with other purging medicines it makes them less hurtful to ye stomach. By being sprinkled on dry it conglutinates wounds, and brings to a cicatrix boils, and represseth them; but it properly healeth exulcerated genitals, and conglutinates ye broken preputia-of boys. It cures also the Condylomata, and ye chaps of ye seat being mixed with sweet wine. And it stops ye fluxes of blood that come from Hemorrhoids, and it brings to a cicatrix ye pterygia, takes away blacks and blues, and ye Hypoxia with honey. And it assuageth Scabrities and the itchings of ye eye corners, and ye headache being anointed with acetum and rosaceum on ye forehead and the temples, and with wine it stays ye hair falling off, and with honey and wine it is good for ye tonsils, as also the gums and all griefs in ye mouth. But it is roasted also for eye medicines in a clean and red hot earthen vessel, being kept urned with a splatter until that it is roasted equally....[13]

Pliny used Aloe in the treatment of leprous sores.[14]

In Africa, tribes have used Aloe to treat colds and to eliminate human scent.[15]

Probably brought to the Americas by the Spanish, Aloe has been used for colds, to protect children from insect bites, as a healing gel, for burns, intestinal disorders, ulcers, and kidney and bladder infections.[16]

In the Philippines it was used to treat beriberi sufferers and in Malasia to relieve headaches.[17]

There is little recorded use in Europe of which I am aware. However, this is probably attributable to the climate. Aloe would have had to be shipped from Africa and its effectiveness by the time of arrival is most questionable. If not effective, its use would be quickly discontinued. It has had considerable usage in Russia in recent periods. In this century it has been the subject of Russian medical studies in the areas of dermatological use, respiratory ailments including tuberculosis, gum infection, as a hemostatic agent following tonsillectomy and in improving small intestine function.

I submit that had Aloe not had beneficial healing results, its usage would have been rapidly discontinued in the civilizations I have referenced.

That a plant found in nature has such healing effect should be of no surprise. Over 300 well-known drugs used in medicine today came from plants. Here are some examples. Cortisone was developed from the Mexican yam. Quinine, used in the treatment of malaria came from the bark of the cinchona tree. From curae we obtain the skeletal muscle relaxant used in surgery. A frequently used pupil dilator comes from the belladonna plant. Digitalis, used in heart ailments, was derived from foxglove. Snakeroot provides a sedative for hypertension. Medicines used in treating Hodgkin's disease and childhood leukemia were developed from the Madagascar periwinkle. Morphine comes from the opium poppy and cocaine from the coca plant. From fungus ergot we obtain a drug that stops bleeding in childbirth and relieves migraine headaches.

To me, the great disappointment is that the plant which may contribute more than any other to human welfare, Aloe vera, is so overlooked or hidden by drug companies and governmental administrative agencies.

CHAPTER 4

TESTIMONIES

To the law and to the testimony.
Isaiah 8:20[18]

In courts of law, truth is most frequently established by the testimony of observants we call witnesses. In few areas of which I am aware are there more available witnesses than in the beneficial use of Aloe. I currently have in my files hundreds of such testimonies.

What are the explanations other than the curative value of Aloe vera? Some sophisticated mental pygmies suggest a placebo effect. Considering the widespread variety of ailments we will examine, we would have to be looking at the largest placebo ever created. I wonder if the placebo criers ever reviewed the study made of feline leukemia, a retrovirus similar to the Human Immunodeficiency Virus. Cats infected with the feline leukemia virus (FeLV) were the subject of the study. The disease is the most important severe cause of illness and death in domestic cats. The infected cats experience a wide range of diseases just as do AIDS patients.

About one-third of all feline deaths are FeLV related. There were two studies conducted by Doctors of Veterinary Medicine at the Animal and Medical Hospital, Irving, Texas, and at the Department of Veterinary Microbiology and Parasitology, College of Veterinary Medicine at Texas A&M University.[19] The cats were regularly injected with acemannan, a chemical taken from the Aloe vera plant. Seventy-one percent of the cats in the study survived a 100% fatal disease. Of the results, the veterinary team conducting one of the studies said:

> ....*analysis of the clinical scores indicate that there was a progressive improvement in subjective clinical scores in treated animals.*

> ....*There was an improvement in major blood parameters during the six weeks the cats were under treatment.*

> ....*The results of this study show clearly that Acemannan (from Aloe vera)-treated cats lived significantly longer than the historical controls.*

....The results of only 6 weeks of treatment must be considered dramatic when measured against the usually poor prognosis of this disease.

....The significant improvement in viability as well as the overall health of the treated cats suggest that acemannan (from Aloe vera) is an effective treatment of FeLV infection.[20]

Who told the cats about the marvelous curative history of Aloe vera or that they were even being injected with acemannan (Aloe vera)?

I herein include only a fraction of available testimonies, separated into disease categories.

AIDS

January 30, 1993

Following is a true and accurate account of my personal experience with the AIDS virus and the course

I chose to pursue in its treatment. This information is being shared not to suggest that this regimen will work for everyone but with the hopes that others may find an element of hope in their own battle with this terrible disease.

Having always been an extremely energetic person all throughout my life, I found it quite unusual that during the summer months of 1992 I was continually feeling drained and weak. After just beginning a new job with a major national publication, I was tested and found to be HIV+. My initial medical tests to determine the extent of the illness showed that my CD4 count was at 72, classifying me as having full-blown AIDS. This was in early September, 1992.

Within about three to four weeks of my initial testing, I began to experience symptoms of the advancement of the disease including severe night sweats, a continuous fever of 102+, constant and frequent diarrhea, difficulty in keeping food down, a general loss of appetite and an extreme weakness in my legs often with difficulty in walking. I also began to develop what appeared to be water blisters on various parts of my body, especially my hands and feet. I also had lost approximately 14 pounds within a 3-1/2 week period.

Already a believer of the benefits of natural products and their benefits to the human body, I began taking a cold processed, whole-leaf Aloe vera concentrate (1200 mg/day of the active ingredients—about 2 ounces) and a potassium mineral supplement manufactured by Matol Botanical International called Km (2 1/2 ounces/day) which is formulated from 14 different botanicals. In addition to these, I began to take a combination of herbal extracts from Pure Herbs, Ltd., including myrrh (60 drops/day), broad beans (40 drops/day) and a formulation called B.P.-W containing bee pollen, buckthorn, greasewood, inkberry, peach leaf, prickly ash, red clover, and stillingia (60 drops/day). I also began an intake of bovine colostrum, processed by Sterling Technologies (1 ounce/day), 35% food grade hydrogen peroxide (9-75) drops/day) and a brown powder locally known as Pygmy Dirt. This course of nutritional supplementation began approximately the second week of October.

The next series of diagnostic testing was done during the first week of November. Those results brought back the following positive information. When initially diagnosed by the American Red Cross as HIV+ in early September, it was also confirmed that I tested positive for hepatitis B. The November test results showed no sign of hepatitis

B surface antigen. Even more encouraging was the fact that these early November test results showed a CD4 count of 810.

Physically, I felt much better than I had previously, with a lot of my strength and endurance returning. I still had some mild symptoms of night sweats and an occasional fever. The weakness in my legs and the difficulty in walking disappeared altogether. The blisters had almost totally dissipated and I began to gain much of my weight back.

I continued this treatment of herbal and nutritional supplementation and received my next series of diagnostic testing the second week of December with the good news that all of my blood counts were within acceptable range and with a CD4 count of 1092. By this time, physically I was feeling extremely well and almost back to the healthy, energetic level I had been accus-

tomed to most of my life. Emo-
tionally and psychologically, I was
pulled between the return of my
physical health and the loss of my
job due to my illness and the severe
financial strain it was placing on
my life.

Jim McPherson[21]

Jim Lightinheart, HIV+ for 10
years, was diagnosed with Non-
Hodgkin's Lymphoma in 1990 and
began a course of chemotherapy
and experimental drugs. Facing the
major challenge of this life-threat-
ening disease and the poisons used
to treat it, he committed himself to
learning how to re-establish and
sustain his health. He spent count-
less hours in medical libraries and
in networking to research strategies
for building his body's ability to
heal. Jim was a phenomenal success! His doctors were astounded
as he maintained his weight throughout chemotherapy and required

no hospitalization for complications. In spite of being one of the only two survivors from a group of approximately twelve undergoing the same treatment for lymphoma, physicians only conceded a casual glance at the materials that were literally saving his life.

Early on in his HIV infection, Jim made the personal choice not to use AZT, DDI, or DDC. His broad program of stress management techniques, personal balance, nutritional supplementations, vitamins, herbs and numerous other health measures have allowed his body to be strong enough to successfully fight lymphoma and prevent the progression of his HIV infection to ARC or AIDS. He has now added three ounces a day of whole leaf Aloe vera concentrate to the measures he uses to keep his immune system strong....

As recounted to the author
by Jim Lightinheart[22]

One of the patients...has been on Aloe since the original study and his T-Cells are almost as healthy as yours or mine. (Count from the time he started Aloe went from about 200 to over 750). And he came in with hepatitis B and was nearly dead when he came to me.
                    Terry Pulse, M.D.[23]

CANCER/TUMORS

In October of 92, my son, Stephen Huff, was diagnosed as having a very rare brain tumor, called meningioma. A craniotomy was performed in December to debulk this tumor. We were informed that early diagnosis and total removal of the tumor, as well as surrounding tissue, assures a happier prognosis. This was not to be our case. There was residual tumor left. These tumors continuously grow. There is

---

no on and off switch that triggers them. Radiation can only slow their growth down, but for how long, no one can be sure. There is chemotherapy available for these tumors. My son has had no radiation, only a strong faith in the Lord, dietary changes, and herbs. In June he started taking Aloe "as the Lord hath planted it." He says he feels uncomfortable when he doesn't get it on schedule. He craves it. He has had 3 M.R.I.'s since December of 92—in February, May, and July of 93. To date, there has been no re-growth of the tumor and his right eye, which is totally blind (since they removed part of his optic nerve), appears normal. After the operation, for months, it remained swollen. The doctors said it was from intracranial contents interfering with venous flow. Whatever was interfering, isn't now. You'd never know he has a brain tumor. "With men this is impossible, but with God all

things are possible." Matt. 19:26.
Maryska K. Hinson[24]

*My mother is a diabetic who also
has Alzheimer's disease. She is a
severe arthritic sufferer and a multiple stroke patient with a large
melanoma about the size of a quar-
ter on her cheek. The doctor performed surgery and removed part of
the cancer. He sent her home and
said it would rapidly spread throughout her body. That was in September 1992, and the doctor told us
he felt the melanoma had spread
too far. She began using a whole-
leaf Aloe vera concentrate and
super gel on the open cancer topically, as well as drinking two ounces per day of the whole-leaf Aloe
vera concentrate. The cancer
completely disappeared within a few
weeks to the amazement of her
doctor. By October 1992, her
arthritic pain was vastly reduced.
She is now coherent 80% of her*

waking hours (she was incoherent 90% of the time before she started using Aloe vera). In September 1992 she was taking 60 units of insulin a day. She now requires zero insulin and her blood sugar is within normal limits. In June of 1993 her doctor told us to continue monitoring her blood sugar level but that she no longer requires insulin

Linda McKittrick[25]

This is a quick note to keep you up to date on what events have occurred with me in the past five weeks. First I need to give you some past data:

Two years ago I was diagnosed with inoperable prostate cancer; inoperable because the malignancy appeared on the outside surface of the prostate and therefore there was some possibility of its already having spread to other areas. I elected for radiation which seemed to stop the problem. Then every six months I took a prostatic blood test which indicated rising enzyme production from 66 to 1,350, which occurred four months ago. During that time a tumor was developing in my lymph glands in the neck area. After three months of using Chinese herbs especially formulated for the increased health of my immune system, the swelling receded 60% to 70%. However, the cancer began to spread to another part of my lymph node system and a grapefruit size tumor developed between my lungs in back of the sternum. Another prostatic blood test showed an increased count to 4,500--a 5th stage cancer.

It was at this time that I had heard you speak about whole leaf Aloe vera and its extraordinary proper- ties and I decided to use it. For four weeks I consumed two ounces of Aloe vera concentrate in six ounces of orange juice three times a day. I also took 4000 mg of a good vitamin C. The doctor was prescribing six tablets of flutamide per day presumably to reduce the production of the male hormone testosterone.

One month later all pain and discomfort were gone and my energy level increased dramatically. Another prostatic blood test showed the levels had gone down to 57.1 The X-ray showed a good ninety percent reduction in the tumor between my lungs. The neck tumor had completely disappeared. All this to the amazement of my doctor who hadn't experienced this rapid improvement in his experience.

I am going to continue to take six ounces of whole leaf Aloe vera concentrate daily until the condition appears to be neutralized, then I will taper off to as little as one ounce a day on an ongoing basis.

While I can't prove the validity of the medicinal benefits of Aloe vera, I would urge you to suggest to anyone who has a life threatening physical problem to use it without reservation. My mental attitude has been that I created this problem and that I could discreate it as well. I have not dwelled on this condition or worried about it and have continued to eat healthy foods and exercise as a way of living my life. With much Aloha, I honor you for your efforts and dedication to your fellow mankind.

Robert A. Kohn[26]

(Author's note: Robert Kohn has since informed us that his PSA count is now .8 and the tumor on his lungs has totally disappeared.)

March 18, 1992

The following is a true and accurate description of the benefits Nan

Yannacito has experienced as a result of her use of a whole leaf Aloe vera concentrate.

In April of 1985, Nan was diagnosed as having ovarian cancer, and at that time surgery was performed. Since that time, she has had numerous recurrences of the cancer and numerous surgeries to remove additional tumors. In addition to the surgical procedures, she has received eleven months of chemotherapy and extensive radiation therapy.

In June of 1991, Nan was told that the cancer had gone to her liver. This condition, along with the increased growth of a tumor, which the surgeons were unable to remove during her most recent surgery, and her deteriorating physical condition, resulted in the conclusion that Nan had six months or less to live. Her oncologist determined that Nan should be put under the care of a

---

*hospice since there was no other
treatment which they felt would be
beneficial to her.*

*Nan was admitted to hospice care
and was being cared for in our
home by nurses and home health
aids. Nan was rapidly losing the
use of her legs, which doctors
attributed to either the deterioration
of nerves as a result of the radiation treatments or as a result of the
growth of the tumor pressing on
nerves going to her legs, the exact
cause was undeterminable.*

*She was able to move around the
house only with the aid of a special
walker. She could shower only
with the help of one of the hospice
health aids because she could not
even stand by herself in the shower.*

*At this time she also began experi-
encing problems digesting food and
developed intestinal blockages as
well as problems with her esopha-*

gus. Her diet by this time consisted of jello, baby food, broth, and liquid diet supplements. She also developed a yeast infection in her mouth which was not responding to treatment.

In August of 1991, it was suggested that Nan start taking a good whole leaf Aloe vera concentrate. After a lot of research, suggestions, and recommendations by experts, it was determined that a whole leaf Aloe vera concentrate was what she would take. Nan started drinking one ounce of the concentrate mixed with fruit juice four times a day beginning the middle of August 1991.

I must admit that our expectations regarding any benefits to be derived from the Aloe were not very high and it was tried with a "what do we have to lose" attitude. Approximately two weeks after starting to drink the Aloe concentrate, Nan began to notice that her legs were feeling better and she had more strength in them as well. The physical therapist who was working with Nan at the time was amazed at her progress. Nan continued to regain the strength in her legs and her mobility continued to improve seemingly daily to the point where she no longer needed the walker to move around the house. She did, however, use a cane for a short while, but soon she no longer needed it.

About the same time, Nan began eating a normal diet with no evidence of the prior digestive problems that she had been experiencing. The yeast infection which had plagued her also disappeared. About Oct 1, 1991, Hospice dismissed Nan from their care stating that her health was no longer deteriorating and, in fact, she was improving.

Nan is now able to walk our dogs around the block by herself and quite often joins me when I walk them on weekends in the park. Her diet is completely normal. Although Nan is not free of cancer, her condition is greatly improved and she is able to enjoy a more normal quality of life. Both of us attribute her amazing improvement to the whole leaf Aloe vera which was the only thing she did differently in an effort to improve her condition.

As a sidelight, I also began drinking the Aloe concentrate at the rate of one ounce per day and, after a period of about two weeks, I found that the arthritis in my knees, which had bothered me for a number of years, had all but disappeared. I hope that telling about the positive results that we have experienced through the use of this product will encourage others to try this remarkable product. We sincerely hope

*that the results will be as rewarding
for others as it has been for us.*
Al Yannacito[27]

*The gastroentologist did an HIV test
on me. It came up positive and
they suspected I had liver cancer,
but ... the specialists were not able
to get the liver tissue they needed.
Dr. Pulse did the 5th biopsy under
computer-assisted tomography.
They found 17 tumors in my liver
and gave me four to twenty-one
days to live. I was told that no one
had ever developed liver cancer to
the point I had. They told me to
call my lawyers, my family and my
priest.*

*I started taking Aloe. The one
thing that was constant was this
craving for Aloe. And they documented through CAT scans that my
tumors began to reduce. They
hadn't seen any response in any
medical literature prior to that.*

Now they tell me there is no evidence of the tumors. Everyone in the hospital kept remarking that they'd never seen anything like it.
Michael Arrington[28]

I want to give you my favorable testimonial about whole leaf Aloe vera concentrate.

I am 72 years of age and as long as I can remember I have had lumps in my breasts. Doctors suspected that I might have cancer, and they said that I had fibrous breasts and to be careful. Pressure like that of a mammogram is brutally painful and would leave me with pain and soreness for weeks. X-rays have the same effect.

A few months ago, after your seminar at the 37th Annual Natural Health Convention...I started taking the concentrate 2 ounces twice a day. The very next month my

breasts were free of lumps and have been soft and free of fibrosity ever since. I thank you for this product.
Susanne S. Cooper[29]

This letter is in regard to our telephone conversation of March 16th, 1992 as pertains to my present health situation and the taking of Aloe.

THE PROBLEM

In August of 1991, I began having a cough that would not go away and which continued day and night. I checked into sick call at the local VA hospital where the doctors there began treating me for an allergy. This treatment continued for the months of August, September, and part of October where many different medicines were prescribed and the cough persisted. I lost 20 pounds and was coughing up blood. My patience with these doctors failed in mid-October when I went to a local ENT physician who performed a bronchoscopy. The bronchial examination revealed a tumor about the size of a golf ball at the juncture of the right and left lobes of my lungs. Pathological examination revealed it was a large cell epithelial tumor and I was transferred to Wilford Hall Air Force Hospital in San Antonio, Texas. Further examination at Wilford revealed the tumor extended around and had constricted my esophagus and that the tumor was one millimeter from my aorta. A regime of radiation therapy was started on my chest and back. Three weeks into this treatment, a bone scan was performed and it was discovered that I had a tumor at the head of my left femur which required an operation to implant steel pins into the femur to keep it from collapsing. I lost 68 pounds from 225 pounds down to 157 pounds. The oncology team informed me that I had 6 months to a year to live and informed me to get my lawyer, priest, etc., and get my life in order for preparation to die. They decided to give radiation to the femur and discharge me to home where I was informed I would get weaker and weaker before death. I was weak, and had no appetite and could take nothing but liquids by mouth when they discharged me in mid-January, 1992.

In mid-December some friends brought me an audio tape of a radio interview of Dr. Lee Ritter concerning Aloe Products. I called Dr. Lee and by the end of December I was taking 6 ounces a day of whole leaf Aloe vera concentrate while in the hospital. After discharge I have continued taking the 6 ounces per day of Aloe vera concentrate.... Each day I began to feel better and by the end of February was strong enough to begin taking care of my personal needs. My appetite had increased to the point I was taking hard food. It is now Mid-March, I can't seem to get enough food (eat all day). My energy level is strong enough that I have been mowing the lawn, working (mechanical repairs) on my rider mower, doing the household chores, and generally feel well. I have regained 15 pounds of weight. I am still not able to work more than an hour or two at a time without 10 to 15 minutes rest, but normally my overall feeling is good. I also take carrot juice each day, a mineral supplement, and lots of fruit juices.

On a visit to the oncologist the first week of March, I was informed not to make a re-appointment again unless I was in need of his immediate care.

I am thankful for the Aloe advice and believe it has improved my health to the point that I conclude I will live much longer than the 6 months given me by the doctors unless I die of something other than cancer.

John H. Knox[30]

MULTIPLE SCLEROSIS

At a meeting I attended in Hawaii, a man who had heard our radio show attended our first meeting and bought a bottle of whole leaf Aloe vera concentrate for his wife who he reported was totally disabled from multiple sclerosis. He said that she was unable to move her arms or grasp well enough to even pick up a cup. He attended our fourth meeting and announced that her strength was improving to the point that she could pick up a cup. By the tenth meeting he very tearfully and joyfully reported that her pain had decreased and her strength had improved to the point that she was able to be out of the wheel-

chair and help around the house.
Accounted orally to the author[31]

Nine months ago Helen Knight couldn't walk without falling down, and her doctor said she would never walk normally again. But last Saturday night she went dancing.

Knight, who was diagnosed with multiple sclerosis five years ago, has been drinking Aloe vera juice … for nine months. She says that is what is helping her to live a more normal life.

Her husband, Dan Knight, said, "She was falling down two to three times a day. She's been improving every day since she started taking it."

About one and a half years ago her husband had a serious car accident, and her condition worsened. Her doctor put her on medication to make her feel better but said he could do nothing else for her. He prescribed hand controls for her car, handrails for in the house, and a wheelchair.

"I said no way. And the wheelchair is still in its box. It has never been used," she said.

That was when she found out about a person in Spokane who suffered from MS, had taken the juice and was in total remission.

"But the company doesn't claim to cure anything. Aloe vera helps the body to heal itself. It cleanses the blood and washes toxins from the body," Dan quickly added.

Helen, who drinks Aloe vera daily, said that, before she started taking it, she couldn't do any of the housework or cooking. Her two young daughters did the housework, and

Dan cooked when he got home from his job at Key Technology where he is a welder.

"Now the kids won't do the housework because they know I will," she said.

She said she only uses the crutches now when walking on uneven ground or when she gets extremely tired. The same goes for the hand controls on the car.

The Knights are eager to help other people get the good results that they got.

"It's good nutrition, and that's why it works," Dan said.

"My motto is that I will walk normally again."
<u>The Valley Herald</u>[32]

DENTISTRY

...The patient needed his wisdom tooth extracted, and while the site was getting numb we talked about Aloe. He said his wife's grandmother had married a Native American back in the thirties and had used Aloe ever since. He reported that she is now ninety-seven years old, looks like she is fifty, and acts like she is forty. He suggested that we try whole leaf Aloe vera concentrate on his wound.

I irrigated the socket with the whole leaf Aloe concentrate and after the sutures were in place, I filled the socket with Aloe gel. That evening I called to see how the patient was doing. His comments were that if his tongue didn't feel the space he would not be aware that anything had happened. He continued to apply Aloe for that week and, when it came time to remove the sutures, the area appeared pink and healed

---

over. I was quite impressed.

We have since used whole leaf Aloe vera concentrate for all surgeries with uniformly gratifying results. One person among many, Mr. Harold Garns, wrote, "I suppose it is unnatural for a patient to tell a dentist that he feels he had not even been treated by him. I honestly feel as if I had not been in your chair. I never felt any pain at any time, nor any discomfort after leaving your office."

What makes the letter so rewarding is that we worked on Mr. Garns for two plus hours, removing numerous teeth, performing bone recontouring, and inserting an upper immediate denture. The checkup the next day showed some mild hematomas, but little swelling. The tissue was a healthy pink. I have not had to prescribe pain medication, except

*for one very drug-oriented patient,
in four months.*
James Harrison, D.D.S., F.A.G.D.[33]

YEAST INFECTION

*For years I have had vaginal yeast
infections. Medicines have not
done any good. Several years ago
I started taking whole leaf Aloe
vera concentrate both orally and as
a douche. Within a couple of
weeks my yeast infection had
cleared up and, ever since, I have
been able to control yeast infections
with Aloe vera.*
Susan Ritter[34]

SINUS/ASTHMA

*Several years ago I purchased a
bottle of whole leaf Aloe vera concentrate. I was a thirty-seven year
old cosmetologist suffering from a
severe sinus infection. I had missed
several days of work and had even*

gone for medical treatment.... Of course I was put on antibiotics, and after two weeks of such treatment, I was worse than ever and now had a rash all over my face and body, which I believe was caused by the antibiotics.

It was at this time my client referred me to your office. She had a sinus problem which had cleared fast with whole leaf Aloe vera concentrate. On the way home I took my first dose and within ten minutes my sinuses had started to clear. In five days the awful pressure and mucous had cleared up and within a week I was back to normal, or should I say <u>better</u> than normal.

I feel better now than I have in years with plenty of energy. Also my allergies are not bothering me. Normally this time of year (April and May) my allergies are <u>terrible!</u> At first I took three ounces daily—morning, noon and night. Now

---

I just take one ounce daily--one-half ounce morning and one-half ounce at night. Whole leaf Aloe vera concentrate has been a life saver for me. Thanks for such a remarkable product.

Jack E. Boyles[35]

...I have had asthma real bad. I carried all kinds of pills with me all the time but no more...[I] never got a cold or flu this last year. (Attributed to the use of whole leaf Aloe vera concentrate).

Jim Younglund[36]

MISCELLANEOUS

After four months of being bedridden and in extreme pain, I ventured to a health conference in Pasadena, California, in search of a cure or remedy for my affliction, Interstitial Cystitis. Because of the disease, my bladder had no lining to protect it and had shrunk and could only hold a few ounces of liquid. It was covered with burns and bleeding ulcerations from the acidic urine pouring over its unprotected tissue continuously. The nerves in the bladder, making contact with the lower back, left me almost totally debilitated from an extreme pain which can only be understood by someone who has had their back out or damaged in some way.

When I arrived at the conference I was hopeful that I would find (out of all of the many knowledgeable providers of holistic alternative healing methods) someone with a product that could alleviate my devastating symptoms. Of all the people I spoke with, only one even knew what the disease interstitial cystitis was, Dr. Lee Ritter. He informed me about the valuable effects of the burn plant, Aloe vera, and warned me about the many impostors on the market. I pur-

chased some of the freeze-dried whole leaf capsules from a reputable company that Dr. Ritter directed me to and I promptly took two capsules. What he told me made sense, but I was skeptical and continued to inquire about other modalities that could possibly help.

It was not until the next morning when I woke up with none of my old symptoms that I realized how important my talk with Dr. Ritter had been. He had led me to a remedy that gave me back the quality of life that I had left behind years before. Once again I could eat the foods that I had loved and was able to venture out into the world without the fear of not being able to find a rest room. The pain in my back had been totally alleviated and my bladder pain disappeared. Instead of holding mere ounces, my bladder began holding more volume and for longer periods of time.

I have to admit that, in an effort to reduce cost, I tried several very well-reputed Aloe vera products on the market, but in all of the cases, my painful symptoms returned almost immediately. In the last ten months I have continued to have the same success with the good Aloe vera product and, even though I know it has not so far been a cure, it has been a wonderful, soothing bandage on my wounded bladder. I know now that no matter what the cost, you get what you pay for. The other products might have seemed like a better deal, but certainly they were not a better value.

In addition to alleviating all of my IC symptoms, my arthritis disappeared about a month after I began taking the aloe. What a plus! I have been given my life back, and for that I sincerely thank Dr. Ritter for his guidance.

Jill M. Wood[37]

[Author's note: I am informed that
interstitial cystitis patients have a
20% suicide rate and over an 80%
divorce rate. The constant pain and
trauma make sexual relations almost
impossible.]

*A few years ago, I was diagnosed
by a leading M.D. as having Paget's Disease, which is a deterioration of the bone marrow.   The
abnormal bones caused me incredi-
ble pain. They were massive and
concentrated in my hips, pelvis, and
the back of my head.*

*The doctor said to me, "Go home
and buy yourself a wheelchair
because you'll need it.   There is
nothing to be done. You have an
incurable and hereditary disease."*

*I went to the Mayo Clinic and was
put on a medication called Caldi-
tonia. I dropped to 119 pounds. It
made me deathly ill.   The Mayo*

doctor then put me on Didronel, which did slow it down. But the side effects were worse than the disease. I had to take 4 or 5 pain-killers per day. I had no relief and very little sleep.

Then an article in a medical journal from England was brought to my attention. It stated that research had determined that Paget's disease is caused by a canine distemper virus. I remembered that when age 13 or 14 I had held a dog with distemper. And I asked my brother who is a nutritionist if he knew of anything that would kill that virus.

He put me in touch with a lady who shipped me two bottles of whole leaf Aloe vera concentrate. I took it first thing in the morning and at night before retiring.

Four days after taking the Aloe, I noticed that the pain had gone. I have had no pain since. It's the

*only thing I have ever found that
has helped.   Concentrated liquid
whole leaf Aloe vera saved my life!
I take it regularly. The disease is
still present, but in remission. And
I feel great!*
H. Gordon Oliver[38]

*I recently had an experience with
an Aloe vera product that might
interest you. For about a year and
three months I suffered greatly with
a severely damaged rotator cuff,
left arm. During this time, my
personal physician provided me
with the full course of treatment: X-
rays, MRI, physical therapy, and
medication.   The result was that
after all the treatment and many
months, I was still unable to lift so
much as a glass of water with my
left arm or to move it in any direction (with a few exceptions) without
a great deal of pain.*

About fourteen months into the damaged rotator cuff, someone told me that it might help if I were to drink Aloe vera. I never heard of such a thing, but this person assured me it was being done and reasoned that since Aloe vera was a healing agent, it might help my arm. So I checked around for a good brand of Aloe vera and finally found a reputable whole leaf Aloe vera concentrated product. I ordered four bottles of the "drink" version. (They also have capsules).

It arrived and for a few weeks I did not bother to open the bottle. Then, at one point, I found myself working in my home office for about a week and a half and decided to give the stuff a try. I drank three ounces of the Aloe vera concentrate a day, in divided doses. After a few days, I noticed that my arm was less painful and that I was able to lift more weight without excruciating pain.

I left home for a business trip and did not take any of the whole leaf Aloe vera concentrate along. After about three days on the road, I found my arm was again painful and I was unable to lift anything. When I returned home I began the three ounces a day routine again. Within three days my arm was noticeably improved. I left for another trip, again taking none of the product along. After three days my arm was hurting much more than before.

I decided the stuff just might be making a difference. Upon my return from that last trip, I went on three ounces a day until I had consumed two bottles. After the first bottle, the pain was much less severe and the arm grew stronger. By the time I finished the second bottle, the pain was gone and has not returned and my arm is much stronger.

Norman Shawchuck, PhD
University of Chicago[39]

I have been drinking whole leaf Aloe vera concentrate since the last of December. My cholesterol was 279. The first of April it was 235. Dr. Jameson told me he did not know why it had gone down. I told him it was drinking aloe vera. "Well if it helps stay with it." I had no more headaches. I have my wife and a lot of friends on it and it works great. I am 69 years young and take no drugs.

Jim Younglund[40]

In this chapter of testimonies I have included only those where I knew either the individual with the symptoms, the treating doctor, or someone close to the individual. I have not included the hundreds of testimonies included in books written by other individuals.

The printed testimonies available in other publications include AIDS, acne, arthritis, athlete's foot, bedsores, blisters, boils, bruises, burns, including radiation burns, diarrhea, eczema, fungus infections, gall bladder infections, headaches, hemorrhoids, herpes, skin disorders, prostate problems, ringworm, sunburn, teeth and gums, ulcers, heart conditions, and numerous other disorders.

The following is a listing of the diseases and ailments where Aloe vera has been applied:

A

abrasions, abscesses, acne, allergies, alopecia areata (loss of hair), aplmar eczema, anemia, arthritis, asthma, athlete's foot, AIDS, arterial complications

B

bites, blemishes, blisters, blood pressure, brain compensation, brown skin spots, bruises, burns, boils, bursitis, bad breath, bladder infections

C

cancer, carcinoma, chicken pox sores, canker sores, cold sores, constipation, candida, colds, coughs, colitis, carbuncles, colic, contusions, cystitis, chemotherapy, cuts, cysts

D

dental treatment, deodorant, dermatitis, diabetes, diaper rash, digestive conditions, dry skin, dandruff, denture sores, drug abuse

E

earache, eczema, edema, erysipelas, epidermitis, Epstein-Barr virus, exanthema,

F

fever, frost bite, fungus infection

G

gums, growing pains, gingivitis, glaucoma, gangrene

H

headaches, heartburn, hemorrhoids, heat rash, high blood pressure, herpes zoster/simplex 1, hepatitis

I

infections, insect stings and bites, insomnia, itching, impetigo, inflamed joints, indigestion

J

jellyfish sting, jock itch, jaundice, joints

K

kidney infection, kidney stones, kraurosis vulvae, keratosis follicularis

L

lacertions, leg ulcer, lichen ruber planus, laxation, leprosy, laryngitis, lupus, liver ailments, leukemia, Lymes disease

M

measles, menstrual discomfort, mouth problems, muscles cramps, multiple sclerosis, mouth irritations, moles

N

nerve damage, neurodermatitis, nocturnal incontinence, nausea

O

onchocerciasis, odors, oxaena, otitis externa

P

pain, peptic ulcer, periodontosis, pils, poison ivy, poison oak, poison summac, pruritus vulvae, psoriasis, pinworms, pancreas

R

ringworm, radiation burns, radiation dermatitis, rashes

S

scalds, scars, schorrhea, scratches and scrapes, sinus, skin cancer, skin care, staphyloma, stinging nettle, stings, stomach disorders, stretch marks, strokes, sunburn, sprains, seborrhea, sore throat, shingles, staph infections, sciatic nerve, sickle-cell disease

T

throat soreness, thrush, tonsillectomy, tuberculosis, thyroid deficiency, tendinitis, trachoma, tumors

U

ulcers, ulcerated skin lesions, urticaria,

V

varicose veins, vaginitis, venereal

sores

W
welts, wounds, wind burn, warts

X
X-ray burns

Y
yeast infections

Z
zoster

Should the reader desire more testimonies I would recommend the following books:

Edith L. Ace, *Healing with Aloe vera* (Pataskala, Ohio: Ace Publications, 1979)

Bill C. Coats, R.Ph, *The Silent Healer* (Bill C. Coats, 1979).

R. Prevost, Compiler, *The Amazing to Ancient Plant, Aloe vera* (Lemon Grove, California: R. Prevost, 1975).

Max B. Skousen. *The Aloe vera Handbook* (Max B. Skousen).

Cheryl Kramer, RN, *Aloe Vera, the Miracle Plant* (Ostrander, Ohio: Cheryl Kramer Publishing Enterprises, 1988).

John Heinerman, *Aloe Vera, Jo-Joba and Yucca* (New Canaan, Connecticut: Keats Publishing, Inc., 1982).

God said that in the mouth of two or three witnesses shall every word be established. It was the number of witnesses that He required in ancient Israel in the most serious cases, such as murder. With Aloe vera we have been given the testimony of literally thousands.

CHAPTER 5

SCIENCE INVESTIGATES

The use of Aloe vera will be the most important single step forward in the treatment of disease in the history of mankind.
H. Reginald McDaniel, M.D.[41]

Actual scientific studies and observations by medical professionals who have used Aloe vera in treating patients are numerous. Since 1990, a considerable number of new studies have begun. I have in this chapter summarized most of those studies which I felt had significance should the reader desire additional information. Several of the studies are of such significance that I want to discuss them in greater detail in this chapter.

The first is a study by O.P. Agarwal, M.D., F.I.C.A.[42] The study was conducted in the 1980's in India and first presented at the annual meeting of the American College of Angiology and the International College of Angiology in San Antonio, Texas on November 5, 1984. The study is significant in that it provided astounding information on the use of Aloe in both the treatment of heart disease and in the treatment of diabetes. Five thousand patients were included in the study, by far the largest number included in any Aloe vera study. The patients ranged in ages from 35 to 65 years of age. The follow-up extended over a five-year period.

Dr. Agarwal's attention was directed to Aloe vera because of its use as an Indian herbal medicine. It has been used as a tonic, purgative, aphrodisiac, anthelminthic, in various pathological disorders, enlargement of spleen, various forms of hepatitis, vomiting, fever due to bronchitis, erysipelas, skin disorders, asthma, leprosy, jaundice, strangury, as a carminative, in various musculoskeletal disorders, menstrual suppression, and various nonspecific disorders.

Aloe vera was mixed with Husk of Isabgol and given to the patients. It would appear that the Husk of Isabgol, which is used in Indian breads, provided fiber.

All of the patients had ischemic heart disease, which was reflected in the form of unequivocal

EKG changes. Of the 5,000 patients, 3,167 were diabetics. Many of the patients had a history of unstable angina. Smoking and the consumption of alcohol were not allowed during the study.

I have always felt that the first effects of Aloe are detected quite quickly. In the study, from the second week most of the patients noted improvement, which was reflected in the disappearance of angina pectoris and a feeling of well-being. From three months to a year all of the patients, except 348, had normal tracing even after treadmill.

In the course of the treatment, normal levels of serum cholesterol, lipids and HDL cholesterol were attained in 4,652 of the patients.

The effects of Aloe on the diabetics were equally astounding. Of the 3,167 diabetics in the study, 2,990 saw their blood sugar values, both fasting and postprandial, start to come down to normal levels. Doctor Agarwal concluded that just under 90% of the 5,000 patients responded positively to the treatment, that is, they experienced beneficial results.

Here is something the FDA should take note of. There were no untoward side effects noticed from the 5,000 patients taking Aloe. Five years after the study, all patients were still living.

Doctor Agarwal concluded that "no Indian plant has ever been tried with such success."[43]

I have said to heart and diabetic specialists, "Please give me the name of any drug or combination of drugs that you are aware of that will produce the same statistical results provided by Doctor Agarwal's study." Most are honest enough to admit they know of nothing even close to being comparable.

The second significant study I want to draw the reader's attention to and comment on is the study by Dr. Terry L. Pulse of 29 AIDS patients. The study was published in the *Journal of Advancement in Medicine*, Winter 1990, Volume 3, No. 4.

I have previously referred to this study because it was what brought me into contact with Aloe vera. The study is personalized for me because I talked with many of the AIDS patients involved. Basically, the patients took 1200 mg of the active ingredient in Aloe vera juice daily as well as nutrient supplements. I quote directly from Dr. Pulse's report of the results, which are unbelievable.

> *No adverse effects attributable to the essential fatty acid capsules were observed nor any side effects of the nutritional supplementation powder nor of the Aloe vera juice. Most patients who were symptomatic reported that within three to five days their energy levels improved, fever disappeared, night sweats stopped, cough decreased or stopped altogether, shortness of breath decreased, lymph nodes decreased in size, diarrhea stopped, strength improved and the only measurable side effect of this particular study was weight gain, which is a desirable effect. There were no biochemical abnormalities noted on SMAC in this particular study. AZT induced anemias improved on this particular regimen.*

Chest x-rays remained normal throughout the study. No changes in EKG from baseline were observed. There was great improvement in all patients to hypersensitivity skin testing at the end of 90 days... Not only did the patients improve clinically and functionally, but their Karnofsky scores improved in 93.1% of the patients at 90 days and in 100% at 180 days. One hundred percent of the modified Walter Reed scores improved at 90 days and 96.4% at 180 days. 51.7% of the patient's T4 helper lymphocytes increased at 90 days and 32.2% at 180 days, with 25% reactive HIV P24 core antigen converted to negative at 90 days and 180 days.[44]

There is really no better determiner of whether a patient is improved than his or her own feeling over an extended period of time. I talked to many of the patients. Those I spoke with were unanimous in their expressions of marked improvement. It would be interesting to see what the study would have reflected had the patients taken an even more concentrated daily amount of Aloe vera. My opinion is that the results would have been even more astounding.

TERRY L. PULSE   M.D., P.A.
FAMILY MEDICINE

PHONE:
(214) 660-1472

2701 OSLER DR., SUITE 2
GRAND PRAIRIE, TEXAS 75051

October 24, 1990

Mr. Lee Ritter
Tripeutics, Inc.
11968 N. Washington
Northglenn, CO 80233

Dear Mr. Ritter:

I have just received the copies you sent of the properly edited and authorized videotape made by Tripeutics,
regarding my use of Immune Essentials Nutritional Support
System, Immune Essentials Fatty Acid Capsules and stabilized
acemannan (Aloe Vera Juice) in treating HIV, ARC and AIDS
patients.

Although you are familiar with my research and have in
your possession one or more abstracts, I thought it would be
helpful for you to know the following:

1. We have recently concluded that 18 months after
initiating the study, of those patients who completed it,
one-half have now gone sero-negative. This is an increase
from the one-third reported at the end of one year.

2. My research has been accepted for publication in
the Journal of Advancement in Medicine and is due to be published in Volume 3, No. 4. As I understand it this should
be the January or February 1991 edition.

Sincerely yours,

Terry L. Pulse, M.D.

TLP/qmm

The third study that I think is most significant wasn't even done on humans. It was done on cats. I refer to it elsewhere in my book to dispel any theories that would attribute Aloe vera treatment to a placebo effect. But here I want to point out the profound results the study reflected for Aloe vera in a terminal viral disease.

The 1991 study was a joint study between the Animal Medical Hospital, Irving, Texas, and the College of Veterinary Medicine, Texas A&M University.[45]

Like AIDS, feline leukemia virus (FeLV) is a retrovirus. Forty percent of cats are dead from the disease within four weeks and 70% within eight weeks. The disease is considered the most important severe cause of illness and death in domestic cats.

The study included fifty cats, all of which were serologically positive for feline leukemia. The cats had failed to respond to conventional treatment. All of the cats were severely ill. The cats were injected regularly with a solution containing acemannan, a product derived from

Aloe vera. The study results reflected:

At the end of the 12-week study, 29 acemannan-treated cats were known to be alive. Two of the original 44 were lost to follow-up and one other died of an unrelated cause, giving a 71% survival rate for those cats that completed the study.

Of 15 cats that died of FeLV-related disease, five died from malignancies or marrow aplasia within nine days of entering the study. These cats can be considered to have been terminal—beyond rescue by any available therapy. Seven other cats died during the 12 week study, and three died within 4 weeks of completing the study. Analysis of 11 historical controls at the same clinic indicated that nine cats died or were euthanized within 2 months, and one other was dead within 5 months of being diagnosed with FeLV.

Two months after completion of the study, a telephone survey of owners was conducted. Attempts were made to contact owners of all surviving cats. Although the owners of five cats had moved and could not be located. Owners of 22 cats were interviewed. One stated that his cat had died 4 weeks after the 12 week follow-up but the remaining 21 cats were reported alive and well.

All owners of surviving cats reported that they were pleased with the results of treatment, stating that their cats had returned to their normal state of activity and were healthy, happy pets (up to 39 weeks after entry into the study). The owner of the cat that died 4 weeks after the study (10 weeks after the final acemannan injection) said that he was encouraged by his cat's having shown improvement during treatment, but that his pet began to deteriorate after the 12-week follow-up.[46]

The study is most significant for two reasons. First, 29 cats that should have, according to all previous scientific studies, been dead, were still alive after 12 weeks and apparently were normal. Second, based upon the study and other documentation, the Department of Agriculture has approved the use of Aloe in treating the disease. This is the first time that internal usage of Aloe in the treatment of disease was approved by a regulatory body. It is a first step in an inevitable direction. Recently, the same laboratory that isolated acemannan from Aloe has obtained approval to conduct a limited study using an Aloe derivative on AIDS patients. One cannot help but believe that the study of cats who were injected with acemannan had some effect upon the FDA which was certainly aware of the feline study. The results of the study being conducted by Carrington Laboratories, a leader in Aloe research, will be closely monitored.

Now take a look at my summary of what I feel are the most relevant studies and observations made on the use of Aloe vera in the treatment of disease.

AIDS

A pilot study reported in 1990 wherein 29 AIDS patients were placed on a supervised regimen of Aloe vera beverage and nutritional supplements. A substantial number of patients' physical condition improved. Energy level improved, fever disappeared, night sweats stopped, cough decreased or stopped, shortness of breath decreased, lymph nodes decreased in size, diarrhea stopped, weakness improved. Hypersensitivity skin testing improved. In 96.4% of the test patients, their Modified Walter Reed Scores had improved at 180 days. Karnofsky scores improved in 93.1%. T4 lymphocytes increased in some patients and, in some, their reactive HIV P24 antigen converted to negative. Terry L. Pulse, M.D., Elizabeth Uhlig, RIE, "A Significant Improvement In A Clinical Pilot Study Utilizing Nutritional Supplements, Essential Fatty Acids and Stabilized Aloe vera Juice." *Journal of Advancement In Medicine*, Winter 1990, Vol. 3, No. 4.

A study of the effects of a carbohydrate compound purified from Aloe vera used with AZT and ACY on AIDS patients. The study concluded that the Aloe vera substance appears to help AZT and ACY block the pathology associated with HIV and herpes simplex virus. Texas A&M University. *AIDS Weekly*, August 5, 1991, p.2.

A study currently being conducted by Carrington Laboratories to indicate what effect acemannan, derived from Aloe vera, has on boosting the immune systems of AIDS patients. The study is noteworthy in that it is being conducted with the Federal Drug Administration's approval. The results of the study should be watched closely.

A preliminary study suggesting that the Aloe vera drug may mimic AZT without toxicity.
A substance in Aloe vera shows signs of boosting the immune systems of AIDS patients and blocking the human immune-deficiency virus spread without toxic side effects. H. Reginald McDaniel, M.D., *Medical World News*, December 1987.

HEART DISEASE/DIABETES

A marked improvement shown in patients taking Aloe vera who had atherosclerotic heart disease, over half of whom were also diabetics. The study demonstrated that Aloe vera had a definite role in controlling the blood sugar level in diabetic patients and in improving the condition of heart patients. The study is significant not only for the results but for the number in the study (5000) and for the period of the study including follow-up (5 years). The study showed a marked reduction in serum cholesterol, serum triglycerides, fasting and postprandial blood sugar levels in diabetic patients. Total lipids and HDL profiles improved. A reduction in the frequency of anginal attacks was reflected in the study. O.P. Agarwal, M.D., F.I.C.A., "Prevention of Atheromatous Heart Disease." *Angiology, The Journal of Vascular Disease,* August 1985, Vol. 36, No. 8, pp. 485-492.

A study of diabetic mice reflecting significant reduction in plasma glucose level when treated with oral doses of Aloe vera. M.A. Ajabnoor, "Effect of Aloes on Blood Glucose Levels in

Normal and Alloxan Diabetic Mice." *Journal of Ethnopharmacol*, February 1990, pp. 215-220.

A report of Aloe vera effectively increasing glucose tolerance in both normal and diabetic rats. F. M. Al-Awadi, K.A. Gumaa. "Studies on the Activity of Individual Plants of an Anti-biotic Plant Mixture." *Acta Diabetol Lat* (Italy), January-March 1987, pp. 37-41.

ARTHRITIS

A study of the use of Aloe vera for therapeutic use in arthritis. R. H. Davis, P. S. Agnew, E. Shapiro. "Antiarthritic Activity of Anthraqui-nones Found in Aloe for Podiatric Medicine." *Journal of American Podiatric Medical Association*, February 1986, pp. 61-66.

BURNS (Including X-ray Burns)

Reported cases and general comments of the beneficial use of Aloe vera in the treatment of

X-ray burns and other burns. Gilbert W. Reynolds, *The Aloes of Tropical Africa and Madagascar*, September 1966, p. 384.

A Russian study that indicates that the use of Aloe vera reduces the sensitivity of the skin to ionization irradiation. Published in Extracts of Aloe, Supplement to Clinical Data Quoted from Max Skousen, *Quotations from Medical Journals on Aloe Research,* p. 10.

A report indicating a noticed relief from pain, and itching, reduction of keratosis and ulceration from radiation burns. James Barrett Brown, M.D., F.A.C.S., *A Cancer Journal for Clinicians*, 1963, Vol. 4, pp. 14-15.

A study of albino rabbits who were subjected to burns and then treated with different ointments. Those treated with substance containing aloe vera showed substantial healing improvement over subjects treated with other ointments. R. Vovatti, M.D., R. J. Brennan, M.D., *Industrial Medicine and Surgery*, 1959, pp. 364-368.

A report on two patients who experienced beneficial healing of X-ray ulcerations where Aloe vera ointment was applied. Adolph B. Loralman, M.D., "Leaf of Aloe vera in Treatment of Roentgen Ray Ulcers," 1936. Quoted from Max Skousen, *Quotations from Medical Journals on Aloe Research*, p. 10.

Aloe vera reported to have a soothing effect on X-ray burns. Archie Fine, M.D., and Samuel Brown, M.D., "Cultivation and Chemical Application of Aloe vera Leaf," 1938. Quoted from Max Skousen, *Quotations from Medical Journals on Aloe Research*, p. 10.

Five patients with radiation ulcers reported relief from pain and discomfort using Aloe vera ointment. Frederick B. Mandeville, M.D.,

"Aloe vera in the Treatment of Radiation Ulcers of Mucous Membranes," 1939. Quoted from Max Skousen, *Quotations from Medical Journals on Aloe Research*, p. 10.

A report that Aloe vera increases the rate of healing from third degree X-ray burns. Tom D. Ravel, B.K. Lowell, Lloyd M. Parks, "Further Observations on the Use of Aloe Vera Leaf in the Treatment of Third Degree X-ray Reaction." *Journal of American Pharmaceutical Association*, 1941.

Experiment where a rabbit was subjected to Beta irradiation. The author concluded that Aloe vera showed a remarkable curative effect upon radiodermatitis in a rabbit. C. C. Lushbaugh, M.D. and D. B. Hale, B.S., "Experimental Acute Radiodermatitis Following Beta Irradiation." *Cancer*, Vol. 6, No. 4.

A discussion of the healing ability of Aloe in burns as an anesthetic, antimicrobial, and anti-prostanoid. John Heggars, M.D., "Myth,

Magic, Witchcraft, or Fact? Aloe vera Revisited," *Journal of Burn Care Rehabilitation*, May 1982.

DERMATOLOGICAL CONDITIONS

A study which indicates that the rate of healing of chronic leg ulcers is improved due to the stimulating effect of the use of an aloe vera gel. The study further reflected beneficial results using Aloe vera in the treatment of acne. M. El Zawahy, M.D., M. Rashad Hegazy, M.D., M. K. Heland, B.Ph., Ph.Ch. *International Journal of Dermatology*, January/February 1973, pp. 68-74.

Study reflects abrasion type wounds heal at least one-third faster than normal healing period when Aloe vera was applied. T.C. Barnes, Hahneunan Medical College and Hospital, *American Journal of Botany*, 1967.

Study indicates that Gibberellin-like substance in Aloe vera is an active anti-inflammatory substance. Conclusion is that Aloe vera inhibits inflammation and adjuvant-induced arthritis. Davis & Maro, "Aloe Vera and Gibberellin: Anti-Inflammatory Activity in Diabetes, *Journal of American Podiatric Medical Association*, January 1989, pp. 24-26.

A report indicating that dermabrasion treated with Aloe vera ointment healed approximately 72 hours earlier than area not treated with Aloe. J.E. Fulton, Jr. "The Stimulation of Post-dermabrasion Wound Healing with Stabilized Aloe Vera Gel-polyethylene Oxide Dressing," *Journal of Dermatological Surgical Oncol.*, May 1990, pp. 460-467.

Preliminary study recommending well-controlled clinical trials indicating evidence of potential beneficial effects in the treatment of radiation ulcers and stasis ulcers in man and burn and frostbite injures in animals. A. D. Klein, N. S. Penneys. "Aloe Vera," *Journal of American Academy of Dermatology*, April 1988, pp. 714-720.

ULCERS

Twelve patients with peptic ulcers were treated with aloe vera taken internally. After 18 months no recurrence of peptic ulcer appeared in any of the patients. Julian J. Blitz, D.O., James W. Smith, D.O. and Jack R. Gerard, D.O. *Journal of the American Osteopathic Association*, April 1963, Vol. 62.

DRUG ABUSE

A study indicating marked improvement in depression levels, anxiety, restful sleep, appetite, nutritional intake, energy and withdrawal symptoms of drug abusers using Aloe vera during recovery from drug abuse. Frank S. Burns, "Substance abuse and the use of Aloe vera products during the early stages of the recovery process," *Spokane Outreach Center Publication*.

DENTAL DISEASE AND USAGE

Ninety-two patients with periodontosis were treated with Aloe vera. Observations included reduced bleeding from the gums, the disappearance of secretions from gum sockets and increased freshness in the oral cavity. S. Levenson and K. Somova, "Therapeutic Stomatology," Irkutah Medical Institute, Russia. Quoted in Max B. Skousen, *Quotation from Medical Journals on Aloe Research*, pp. 29-30.

A report on the use of Aloe vera to alleviate pain and reduce swelling in dental patients. James Harrison, D.D.S., F.A.G.D., "Aloe in Dentistry," *Health Consciousness*, 1992, Vol. 13, No. 1, pp. 19-24.

OTHER INTERNAL DISORDERS

An article discussing how Aloe vera works as an anti-inflammatory agent, its virucidal, bactericidal and fungicidal properties, its effect on the cells of the immune system and its use in the treatment of immune deficiency disorders. John C. Pittman, M.D. *Health Consciousness*, 1992, Vol. 13, No. 1, pp. 28-30.

Observations on the treatment of patients using Aloe vera for esophagitis, gastritis, peptic ulcer, mouth lesions, cold sores, infected gums, sore throat, sinus congestion, irritable bowel syndrome, ulcerative colitis, Crohns disease, vaginitis, lupus, and arthritis. The report indicates the amounts of Aloe used and the methods of application. Lee Cowden, M.D., "Aloe Vera, the Miraculous Healer." *Health Consciousness*, 1992. Vol. 13, No. 1, pp. 25.

Observations regarding the effectiveness of Aloe vera with gastritis and gastric disorders. Robert A. VanHorn, D.C., Stagle Chiropractic Center, Letter dated February 9, 1988. quoted in *Aloe Vera, the Miracle Plant*, Cheryl Kramer (Ostrander, Ohio, 1988). p. 53.

A technical discussion of what constitutes the *best* Aloe vera. Recommends cold-processing or brief exposure to heat. Ivan E. Danhof, Ph.D., M.D., "Aloe Leaf Handling and Constituent Variability." *Aloe Today*, pp. 12-14.

Interview concerning treating patients successfully with Aloe vera for ulcers, arthritis, and multiple sclerosis. Robert Picker, M.D., interview with Maureen Salaman, *Public Scrutiny*, May 1982, Vol. XXVII, No. 11.

CHAPTER SIX

HOW ALOE VERA WORKS

Knowledge is of two kinds. We know a subject ourselves, or we know where we can find information upon it.
Samuel Johnson[47]

The Federal Drug Administration prohibits the prescribing of medicines which they have not approved. Even if I were to recommend how Aloe vera should be used in the treatment of a particular illness or ailment, such advice may be interpreted as the prescribing of a medicine. Further, state laws prohibit anyone not licensed from prescribing certain medicines.

I have no intention of violating federal or state law by recommending the use of Aloe vera in the treatment of disease. In this chapter of my book, I will simply indicate how it appears that Aloe vera works in the human body. I will also describe the way Aloe vera has been used by others to treat injury and disease.

Aloe vera contains at least six antiseptic agents: lupeol, salicylic acid, urea nitrogen, cinnamic acid, phenol, and sulfur. Each of these substances exhibits antimicrobial activity and in my opinion contribute to what I believe to be Aloe vera's infection fighting characteristics.

The lupeol, salicylic acid, and magnesium in Aloe are very effective analgesics (pain killers). Testimonies recount the soothing, pain relieving effect of Aloe when applied topically or taken orally.

Research by Dr. Bill McAnalley at Carrington Laboratories, Inc., indicates that Aloe vera contains a B(1,4)-linked sugar which has been given the trade name *acemannan*. This complex, long chain sugar-linked, acetylated polymannose is an immunostimulator with feedback inhibition. Apparently it binds to a receptor site and activates macrophages which are the cells that command and control our immune system. The macrophages in turn synthesize and secrete monokines at the location where the body disease occurs. The monokines are released in the exact amount required to fight the disease. Monokines include interleukin-1, interferon, prostaglandin-EZ, tumor necrosis factor, and colony stimulating factors.

What is most amazing about Dr. McAnalley's study is that when monokins are synthetically administered, such as by injection or pill, an overdose can result in serious side effects or even in death. But in a manner not fully understood, acemannan eliminates the uncertainty of the dosage. Its mechanism of action in someway deactivates the microphages once a high level of monokines is reached in the blood.[48] There appear to be no side effects from taking very high dosages.

Also found in Aloe vera are the fatty acids, cholesterol, campesterol and B-sitosterol. These fatty acid steroids are known to have anti-inflammatory characteristics. Certainly these chemicals contribute to the treatment of burns, cuts, scrapes, abrasions, and other dermatological conditions. It has been suggested that these substances are beneficial in the healing of rheumatoid arthritis, ulcers, and other internal afflictions.

Researchers claim that Aloe contains the basic

---

materials found in DMSO, a patented chemical that has the ability to penetrate skin tissue, carrying with it desired drugs into the body.[49] Aloe's characteristic abililty to penetrate all seven skin layers would account for its ability to provide pain relief and anti-inflammatory healing when applied topically for muscle damage, arthritis, bursitis, and other similar ailments.

All of the substances that I have mentioned can today be synthesized by drug companies. However, the drug companies cannot duplicate the fine, proportionate balance of these chemical substances, nor can they define or duplicate the manner in which they work upon each other and together. This relationship I like to refer to as synergism. It is this synergism which makes Aloe vera nature's miracle.

The nutrients working together strengthen our immune system which God created to naturally fight disease.

In the recent war in the Middle East, Operation Desert Storm, we only went to war when we had built up forces in excess of those required to do the job. Some have referred to this approach as *overkill*. But it was effective and very quickly so. My observation from those who have experienced the greatest success with Aloe vera is that they operated on the same theory, overkill. And why not? With no known side effects, there appears to be no harm. To those who complain about the cost of using Aloe, my reply is always the same, "Your funeral costs today far exceed a very lengthy period of Aloe vera usage."

Now let's take a look at how Aloe vera has been used, topically and internally. My intention in the remainder of this chapter is not to prescribe the use of Aloe vera. As I have indicated, state and federal laws prohibit my prescribing of Aloe vera as a medicine. My intent is to simply indicate how those who used Aloe vera have related it has helped them.

INTERNAL DISORDERS

In internal disorders ranging from AIDS through cancer, tumors, ulcers, gastrointestinal diseases, multiple sclerosis, bladder infection, asthma, and other internal conditions, Aloe is taken orally. There are several ways to take the Aloe. The

___

method I use is to take the Aloe concentrate
directly. Some who have difficulty with the
taste prefer to mix the drink with another beverage such as orange juice. There are Aloe beverages that can be purchased in health food stores
and from other sources. My concern with the
majority of Aloe vera beverages is that they lack
sufficient volume of Aloe vera's active ingredients to be effective. For further information on
this dilution problem, I refer you to Chapter 7
of this book, *Watch Out For The Frauds*. Aloe
vera can also be effectively taken in powder or
capsule form.

AIDS patients, with what appears to be the most
effective results, take between 1,200 and 3,000
milligrams a day of the active ingredients. The
AIDS patient studies reflect that the patients
spread their level of intake into four separate
consumptions during the day.

Faced with serious health conditions a few years
ago, I started on a regimen of 3,000 milligrams
per day of the active ingredients found in the
whole leaf Aloe vera concentrate. When the

conditions were cured, I continued to take whole leaf Aloe vera concentrate but in reduced amounts.

PROSTATE CONDITIONS

Early treatment consisted of placing a piece of the Aloe vera gel in the rectum, similar to the manner in which a suppository is used. Most current treatments are two-pronged, consisting of taking Aloe orally and also inserting drops of Aloe vera, either in concentrated or diluted form rectally, using a baby syringe.

ARTHRITIS AND OTHER JOINT AND MUSCLE INFLAMMATIONS

Whole leaf Aloe vera is taken internally, undiluted or diluted to suit one's taste, for arthritis and other inflammatory conditions. Again, there appears to be no reason why the dosage should not be comparable to that taken in studies for other internal conditions, i.e. between 1,200 and 3,000 milligrams a day of the active ingredients found in Aloe vera.

VAGINAL IRRITATION

Frequently, vaginal irritation is caused by a yeast infection. In some situations individuals have indicated complete recovery when Aloe vera is taken orally and also used in a diluted preparation as a douche. In other instances a suppository made from the gel has been applied. Sitz baths have also been used.

HEMORRHOIDS

Testimony is replete with the use of Aloe for relieving irritation and itching caused by a hemorrhoidal condition. Similar to early treatment of prostate conditions, the Aloe gel, cut from the plant was directly inserted into the rectum. Some even froze the gel in the form of a suppository to give it more rigidity. Today the same relief is obtained by moistening the troublesome area with drops of the concentrate, with a diluted solution, or with topical cremes and gels.

COLDS AND SINUS CONDITIONS

There appear to be two ways in which colds and

sinus conditions have been treated with Aloe vera. One manner has been by inhaling vapor containing Aloe vera. The other manner has been by taking the Aloe internally, allowing it to strengthen the immune system. The reader might desire to refer to the account of Dr. H. Reginald McDaniel in Chapter 2, *Seeing Is Believing*, when he gave his opinion as to the positive effect of Aloe vera on his residual bronchial condition following pneumonia.

SKIN DISORDERS/TOPICAL APPLICATIONS

Ranging from burns, ulcerated skin and sores through acne, the most common application has been to apply an Aloe vera substance directly to the disorder. Still not uncommon today is the method of removing the peel and aloin and placing the gel, in a wrap, on the condition. New ointments on the market today provide the same benefits, are more readily available and easier to work with.

In most instances, at frequent periods, the skin disorder would be washed and new Aloe again placed on the condition. There are some reports of individuals bathing their entire bodies in an

Aloe preparation.

Some disorders, such as Acne, have been treated both internally and externally in combination, the theory being that the body contains poisonous toxins which contribute to the acne condition. A diluted Aloe concentrate is applied several times a day to the face and other areas where the acne appears. With effective Aloe vera creams and ointments available, they may also be applied.

In cases of rashes, poison oak, ivy and sumac, Aloe vera juice or ointment has reduced the itching and swelling.

SORE THROATS

A diluted Aloe concentrate is gargled as well as taken internally for the purpose of strengthening the immune condition so that the body can fight the infection.

MOUTHWASH

Aloe vera juice in a diluted form is used as a mouthwash. Others feel that in taking the Aloe concentrate orally they obtain the same effect. Bad breath is eliminated as the germs are killed.

EARACHES

Aloe vera juice, which has been warmed, when placed in the ear has been used to relieve pain. Its ability to penetrate skin and membrane, it is felt, allows the Aloe to work on the underlying infection.

DEODORANT

Some people, particularly those allergic to commercial disinfectants, have applied Aloe vera juice or ointment under the arms as a deodorant.

INSECT REPELLANT

Aloe vera juice rubbed on the skin has been used as an insect repellant. There may be some connection between its use as a repellant and its use among native African tribes during game hunts to hide the human smell from the animals.

I end this chapter by repeating observations made elsewhere. I am not aware of any adverse reactions occurring because a person took too heavy a dosage of Aloe vera. I concluded in my own situation that I would use 3,000 milligrams of the active ingredients of whole leaf Aloe vera concentrate daily.

When applying Aloe topically, I would follow the same approach. Further, even where the condition might be considered a topical condition, ranging from acne to a vaginal irritation, if the cause may be even partially an internal infection or disorder, I would take the Aloe internally as well as apply it topically. For the topical application I use an Aloe cream to prevent too great a drying of the skin.

Finally, two cautions. First, in Chapter 7, *Watch Out For The Frauds*, I discuss the frauds in the industry. If your decision is to use Aloe vera in treatment, use an effective brand. I emphasize again, the majority of brands available today do not have sufficient strength (concentrate of Aloe vera) or ingredients (often destroyed or eliminated in processing) to be of any value. The second caution is this, I do not prescribe. I have only indicated the ways in which people have used Aloe vera to treat illnesses and ailments. Consultation with a licensed professional regarding the use of Aloe vera may be appropriate and necessary.

CHAPTER 7

WATCH OUT FOR
THE FRAUDS

That a lie which is half a truth is ever the blackest of lies.

Tennyson[50]

If you take a 10,000 gallon vat and put one gallon of Aloe vera juice in it and then add 9,999 gallons of water, you can advertise that it contains 100 percent pure stabilized Aloe vera. That has been the position of the Food and Drug Administration to date. One FDA representative said to me, "It's not our responsibility to say how much water is in a tomato, an orange or in Aloe vera." There is now some indication that the FDA is going to change their position and require certain levels of Aloe vera to be present. The problem is that the unscrupulous and fraudulent producers and marketers in the industry have taken advantage of the FDA's current position.

Doctor Reginald McDaniel indicated to me that,

of over 200 Aloe vera beverages tested in the mid 1980's, only three contained a sufficient content of Aloe to be of any medical value to the consumer. The tests that I have run would indicate that, even today, *less than one percent* of readily available brands contain acceptable levels of Aloe vera.

The president of a large multi-level marketing company that sells Aloe vera was at my office and we were discussing the value of selling top quality Aloe vera products. During the conversation he became very disturbed about this conversation and suddenly jumped to his feet, bombastically pounded his fist down on my desk, and said, "Product doesn't mean a *_*_*. All that matters is that you have a good marketing plan. People are only interested in money. I could sell bottled water or recycled paper. The bottom line is money."

A leader in the Aloe industry and owner of a private label Aloe beverage company told me when I remarked that his product did not contain enough Aloe to be of any value, "Lee Ritter, for the price these people are willing to pay, you can't bottle anything but water."

I replied, "Then don't bottle anything."

The harm that is done by putting out an Aloe vera beverage with only diluted, minute quantities of Aloe vera in it is tremendous. The consumer receives no benefit and comes to the conclusion that Aloe vera doesn't work. In every case where someone has told me that Aloe vera did not do them any good, the story has been the same. There were insufficient quantities of Aloe vera in the drink.

The following story is an example of the harm that can occur. A gentlemen came to me about three years ago suffering from Epstein-Barr virus, candida and herpes. From the top of his head to the tips of his toes, his body was covered with sores. Puss emitted from several of the lesions. He told me that he spent $168,000 over a three-year period seeking conventional medical treatment and his condition had only gotten worse. I asked him if he'd tried Aloe. He replied, "I'm taking Aloe right now and it hasn't helped." I asked him the brand. It is one of those listed on the chart in this chapter. The tests by Ivan E. Danhof, Ph.D., M.D. at North Texas Research Laboratory indicated that the brand contained *no* Aloe at all. When I advised the gentleman of this, he indicated that previously he had tried another brand, also unsuccessfully. Again, an identification of that brand indicated insufficient quantities to be of substantial value. I suggested that, if he was going to use Aloe vera, then he should use a brand that had sufficient quantities to do some good. I told him my theory for approaching the problems aggressively with high daily intake of Aloe concentrate. I reminded him that you don't fight a forest fire with a garden hose. If I were in his shoes I would take a whole leaf Aloe vera concentrate.

Within a few days the man noticed a marked improvement. He told me that he even put it in the bathtub and snorkeled to make sure it covered his whole body. He used it both internally and topically. Within three months there wasn't a sore remaining. His doctor called me and said, "His body was even worse inside. I doubted if he would have lived another year and now he's completely recovered."

The blame for selling worthless products should not be placed on the health stores for the most part. The distributor tells them that it is a good product and they purchase it for their customers. They don't have any idea how to test it. Even the label says, "One Hundred Percent Pure, Stabilized Aloe Vera." Remember, that label does not tell you how much Aloe vera is in the bottle, just that what is there is pure. It's the producer and distributor who incur my wrath. They know exactly what they are doing. There are over 1,000 brands of Aloe vera available on the market, most of which are privately labeled by about 20 producers. I suggested to one of these suppliers that he knew better and had a moral responsibility not to bottle a worthless product. His reply was that the purchasers prepared their own label and he just put into it what they requested, all of course for a profit.

I recently visited a large international health food distributor. They knew who I was and that I tested brands to determine Aloe vera content. I already knew that the brand they distributed was of little or no value. When I told them that I would like to buy several bottles, they indicated that they had none available. They just didn't want me exposing what they were doing.

As I have indicated, one brand, *George's Always Active Aloe*, tested by Dr. Danhof, indicated that there was no Aloe vera present. One testing determiner is the presence of polysacchrides. I called the owner, George Warren, and asked him about his product. He replied that he removed all of the polysacchrides. I advised him that every scientific study indicated that it was the polysacchrides, the long sugar chains, that were the source of much of the benefit found in Aloe. His answer was that science didn't know what it was talking about and that he had another theory. When I asked him what that theory could possibly be, he refused to tell me. The story became even more bizarre when he told me that he had observed the Roadrunner pecking holes in only some of the Aloe vera plants and, from this observation, he determined which plants were productive. The indication was that this is how he obtained the plants he used. When I asked him where his Aloe vera acreage was, inasmuch as the area he had referred to in our conversation had been destroyed by frost several years ago, he again refused to give me any answers. Anyway, as to George's Always Active Aloe, he advertises that it tastes like spring water, with no preservatives or chemicals added.   Dr. Ivan E. Danhof, Ph.D., M.D., concluded his report of George's Always Active Aloe by stating:

> *This product indicates it contains no preservatives. This is a distillate of aloe leaves; all that come over in the steam is water and a few volatile materials which accounts for the tiny amount of total solids. <u>This material looks like water, tastes like water, and, indeed, is water.</u>* (emphasis added)[51]

Some of the more sophisticated frauds are now adding a non-Aloe vera substance just to fool the simpler testing for Aloe vera contents. More sophisticated testing to detect these frauds must be performed by trained technicians in laboratories.

Senator Orrin Hatch recently spoke to the health food industry. He indicated that the greatest threat to them is their inability to control themselves, particularly those who deliberately misrepresent their product or its potential value.

Remember carefully the words of Dr. H. Reginald McDaniel, the Chief of Pathology at Dallas-Ft. Worth Medical Center, "Make absolutely sure that what you are drinking is, in fact, Aloe vera juice and not water."[52]

It was the dilution problem that brought me to the conclusion that the purchase of a concentrate was the best and safest approach. When I made this recommendation, there were no concentrates available on the market to the consumer. Now there are several, of which many are mislabeled. With a concentrate you know how much Aloe vera you are taking, either in concentrate form or mixed by you in a beverage of your choice.

There are other problems besides that of dilution in purchasing a product. How is the Aloe prepared? Much of the chemical value of the Aloe vera plant is found in the leaves. However, just under the leaves is a yellow sap called Aloin. This substance is a very strong laxative and needs to be removed. The plant must be subjected to a process that grinds the leaves, removes the harmful substances chemically and by filtration, and then treats the Aloe to insure that it will stabilize in a useable condition that

maintains the desired levels of active ingredients. This process is complicated. Aloe vera
juice is, on the average, 99 percent water. All
the chemicals together then amount to no more
than one percent of the Aloe leaf. In that one
percent there are over two hundred different
ingredients. The manner in which they work
on each other and together, which I call synergism, is still not scientifically understood.
Thus it is essential that all of the ingredients
be retained and not altered.

Because carbohydrate and glycoprotein constituents of Aloe are prone to rapid spoilage, the
Aloe vera must be subjected to some method of
preservation. The two accepted methods are
heat treatment and cold processing which em-
ploys chemical preservatives. The heat treatment is somewhat akin to pasteurization. Studies indicate that long exposure to heat produces
significant losses in active constituents. In my
experience, while it is the most costly, cold
processing is the best process for retaining the
greatest benefit from the Aloe vera ingredients.

Aloe vera misrepresentation is also prevalent in
the cosmetic industry where Aloe vera is an

included ingredient. Many manufacturers indicate in large letters that their product contains Aloe. However, when you look at the ingredients, Aloe is usually the last or next to the last ingredient mentioned. The key to remember is that the ingredients must be listed in the order of their percentage volume in the product. Most of these cosmetic products list deionized water as the first ingredient. That should be a pretty good indicator as to what is the most voluminous ingredient. To be of benefit, Aloe should be the first or near the first of the products listed.

Consult with experts and talk with people who have had success using Aloe vera. It's the best way to determine that you are getting an Aloe vera product that works.

I end this chapter by including a chart I have prepared indicating the content and price of different Aloe vera products available on the market today. Read the chart and see which are the genuine, which are the frauds and which are the best buys for your money.

The brands listed in the chart are shown in order

from the least to the most expensive for 1,200 milligrams of mucopolysaccharides.

BRAND	DAILY COST per 1200 of MPS	AVERAGE mg/L
Aloe Master Int'l. 10X	$1.77	17,191
R Pur Aloe 15X	$5.40	6,660
Coats Aloe Int'l	$7.03	2,220
Lametco	$8.82	4,080
Forever Living Products	$12.68	1,420
Catherine's Choice	$74.78	160
George's	no aloe detected	no aloe detected

CHAPTER 8

ABOUT AIDS

*Aloe is to an AIDS patient such as insulin is
to a diabetic.*
                    Terry L. Pulse, M.D.[53]

A separate chapter on AIDS may seem like a
digression from Aloe vera, which is the subject
of this book.   However, because it was my
interest and concern for AIDS patients that led
me to Aloe vera and because I have some very
strong feelings and views about what is happen-
ing, I have devoted this separate chapter to the
subject.

Technically AIDS is really a stage of the infection progression of a virus which is known as
the Human Immunodeficiency Virus, to which
we give the common name HIV.   Even more
technically, medical scientists are discovering
different strains of the HIV virus which they
label accordingly, HIV-1, HIV-2, etc.

The HIV virus was first identified in 1981 as a
mysterious syndrome. A cluster of rare diseases

had suddenly become common in homosexual men.

From following carefully the lives of individuals infected with HIV, a six stage classification was established. This is the Walter Reed scale that Dr. Terry Pulse refers to in his study of AIDS patients who took Aloe vera. Simplified, the stages are:

STAGE	SYMPTOMS
0	Exposure to the Human Immuno-deficiency Virus.
1	Identification of the disease, normally by detecting the presence of antibodies.
2	The development of chronically swollen lymph nodes.
3	A persistent drop in the T4-cell count, usually from the normal 800 T4-cells per cubic millimeter of blood to approximately 400 T4-cells.

4   A failure to respond to skin tests that measure delayed hypersensitivity.

5   The T4-cell count is normally below 200. There is a total absence of hypersensitivity. There is the first evidence of a breakdown in all-mediated immunity. The patient normally develops Thrush and other viral or fungal infections of the skin and mucous membranes. There is a severe decline in the immune system.

6   The stage defined as full-blown AIDS. The T4-cell count is 100 or less. Patients develop a variety of diseases such as pneumonia, fungal infection, Karposi sarcoma and other cancers.

At this time, with the FDA approved treatments, one hundred percent of those in stage six will

---

die within a few years, almost all within two years.

The Human Immunodeficiency Virus works slowly over a period of between 7 and 14 years. Based upon statistical patterns, the whole continent of Africa where HIV is the most prevalent could be wiped out within a short number of years. A slower but similar pattern could occur in the United States, in fact throughout the entire world.

There are many things that we do not know about AIDS. We do not really know how it is transmitted. We do not completely understand how its retrovirus activity destroys T4 and other disease fighting cells in our immune system. We do not even know where it originated. The most common theory is that it is a cross-over virus, that is, it jumped from another species to man. African Green Monkeys are the most suggested origin. Another French study indicates that a similarity exists between the sequence of genetic material found in a virus in a chimpanzee in Gabon, Africa, and the Human Immunodeficiency Virus.

A theory propounded by Robert B. Strecker, M.D., a practicing internist and gastroenterologist who also holds a Ph.D. in pharmacology, presently has my attention and appears to me to be the most plausible.[54]

Doctor Strecker indicates that the Human Immunodeficiency Virus resembles the Bovine Leukemia Virus found in cattle and the Visna Virus found in sheep. The molecular weight of the viruses is the same. He theorizes that the initial source of the cross-species infection originated with smallpox vaccine batches. Doctor Strecker is not alone in this idea. While it received very limited press coverage in the United States, the theory received much wider publication in Europe. Doctor Strecker states that dating backward from the time of the identification of AIDS in Africa to the approximate time of infection, there is a period of time which corresponds with the period when the World Health Organization performed widespread smallpox vaccinations in the exact location in Africa where AIDS later first broke out.

The smallpox virus from which the vaccine is processed is obtained by scraping infected scabs from cattle and then collecting the drippings. Doctor Strecker indicates a strong probability that Bovine Leukemia Virus was present in the batches and not destroyed in the vaccine processing. On whether its presence was intentional or unintentional, he does not comment.

The widespread infection in the Haitian population is attributed by Dr. Strecker to the presence of 10,000 Haitians workers who received the questionable vaccine while in Africa and subsequently returned to Haiti. As to the outbreak of HIV infection among homosexuals in centers such as San Francisco and New York, the doctor does not yet have an answer but indicates there may be a similar cause from some government program such as a pilot hepatitis immunization program.

No one has found a cure for AIDS. The problem is complicated because the virus appears to mutate in each infected individual. Every Human Immunodeficiency Virus that is isolated appears to be different. The differences may prohibit the development of a vaccine.

AZT is the principle drug approved by the

Federal Drug Administration for the treatment of HIV positive patients. The studies that gave rise to its quick approval are very questionable and not totally accurate in my opinion. The drug AZT may in fact kill the patient as it does damage to kidneys, the liver and the neurological system and develops anemia in patients. It is so toxic that over 50% of AIDS patients cannot tolerate the drug. Whether AZT prolongs or shortens life is most questionable.

Aloe vera has no toxicity. It damages no organisms. I have never heard of anyone not being able to tolerate taking Aloe. The Pulse study unquestionably indicates that advanced stages, as reflected by the Walter Reed scores, were reversed by patients who took Aloe vera. Which really prolongs life, AZT or Aloe vera?

CHAPTER 9

WHAT YOU SHOULD KNOW ABOUT THE FOOD AND DRUG ADMINISTRATION

And thus Bureaucracy, the giant power wielded by pygmies, came into the world.
Honore de Balzac[55]

The Food and Drug Administration is an agency of the United States Department of Health and Human Resources. It was created in 1928 by an Act of Congress to protect the public against harmful, unsanitary, or falsely labeled foods, drugs, cosmetics, or therapeutic devices.

It is not with the FDA's original purpose that I find the fault. Rather it is with the bureaucratic and sometimes incompetent expansion of that responsibility that I am critical. I find it difficult to believe that the FDA's primary concern and loyalty is to the citizens of the United States. They approve drugs that in my opinion should never be approved, while prohibiting the sale for medical purposes of drugs that are beneficial.

The FDA has approved the use of Accutane for treatment of acne. By the agency's own admission it is believed that the drug has caused hundreds of babies to be born with birth defects.[56] The drug can damage the kidneys and liver of patients. Aloe vera does no damage, and based upon the testimony of those who have used it as a treatment for acne, it clears up even the most serious of conditions. And yet the FDA will not approve its use as a treatment for acne because Aloe vera has not gone through the FDA's very expensive study and review process. Unless the government funds the process, it will never be approved because treatment with Aloe vera, a drug freely available in nature, cannot be patented. A private company that cannot obtain proprietary rights to Aloe vera is not going to put up the millions of dollars required to obtain approval.

The FDA could solve the problem. It could recommend to the National Institute of Health or other government programs that they conduct the studies. I, as well as others, have certainly submitted to them sufficient information to cause them to act if they had the interest of the public as their priority. In the appendix of this book I have included the correspondence regarding the information I submitted the FDA. They indicated that they did not have the time nor the funds to investigate or review the documentation I sent to them on Aloe vera.

Here is another example of the FDA's blundering. AZT, which is used in the treatment of AIDS patients, is one of the most toxic drugs ever approved. It blocks DNA synthesis in the body, destroys bone marrow, and does extensive kidney and liver damage, and the patient dies. And yet the FDA approves its use for AIDS patients. Doctor William Campbell Douglass, M.D., published an article in which he states that, in order to hurry the testing through because of the pressure on the FDA, they tampered with the test results. False data was retained and included in the study. Midway through the study, the trials of patients with AZT were abruptly terminated and the FDA announced that AZT had miraculously preserved lives and that it would be unethical to withhold the drug from AIDS patients. The premature termination of the trials destroyed the study design.[57] Says Dr. Douglass,

> *After the Phase II trials were over,*
> *most of the misled and desperate*
> *patients decided to begin or contin-*
> *ue using AZT as their "only" hope.*
> *At this point the miracle stopped.*
> *The patients kept right on dying*
> *and, after 21 weeks, 10% of the*
> *patients on AZT were dead.*[58]

I would defy the FDA to compare the Pulse study of AIDS patients taking Aloe vera with any study of patients taking AZT. I believe that patients following the treatment in the Pulse study will always be better off and there is no damage from Aloe vera to the body.

One has to question the motives of the FDA when in 1989 a Congressional Committee heard testimony about payoffs to officials at the Food and Drug Administration to obtain FDA approval of certain drugs. As a result of the testimony, four FDA employees went to prison for accepting bribes. One of the key witnesses against the FDA has since indicated that he has been punitively harassed by the FDA through increased inspections and inexcusable delays in getting approval for drugs manufactured by his company.[59] In 1991 agents representing the FDA and other government agencies swooped down on the offices of Sporicidin, Inc., a legitimate company manufacturing spore killing products. The government seized the products, ordered a stop to sales, and filed a complaint alleging the products were *adulterated and mislabeled*. The FDA issued public statements accusing the company of false and misleading advertising and stated that the products were ineffective.

When all the facts were made available, what turned out to be defective were the government's tests and the regulators' misunderstanding of basic chemistry. Four months after the government's arbitrary action, they backed down, consenting to allow the product back on the market with no changes. But the damage had been done. Business had been lost. Buyers who had heard the FDA's earlier erroneous statements would be dubious about buying.[60]

The FDA told me I couldn't talk about the

benefits of Aloe and then sell the product because the FDA's approval procedures had not
been completely followed. So, now all I do is
share the experiences of others and report on
available scientific studies. I leave to the reader
the determination of whether he or she will try
Aloe vera. In my mind, it is tragic to look at
what the FDA could do to help if they would
shed their narrow, well lobbied perspective on
non-medicinal alternatives. I have included in
the appendix to this book a copy of my correspondence with the FDA. Their statement that
they are unaware of any scientific studies which
reflect that Aloe vera is safe and effective in the
treatment of disease is untrue. Hypocritically,
the government claims to worry about the safety
of Aloe vera while approving AZT and govern-
ment-funded abortions which kill fetuses and
sometimes mothers.

CHAPTER 10

QUESTIONS
AND
ANSWERS

It is better to know some of the questions than all of the answers.

Old Saying

As I travel the country, I continue to have questions asked of me. In this chapter I have tried to include the more frequently asked ones as well as some that should be asked. You will see that I don't have all the answers. Only God has that prerogative.

QUESTION
Will using Aloe vera cure my condition?

ANSWER
I don't know. It is dangerous to talk in terms of cure and I won't. Try it and see what beneficial results you receive. I know of no one who has been harmed by Aloe vera. I know of so many that testify to miraculous benefits. I know the

medically identified properties of the ingredients found in Aloe vera. I know it has worked for me.

QUESTION
How much Aloe should I take?

ANSWER
First, you must know the Muccopolysaccharide (MPS) count in the brand you are taking. Then you should take an amount that is equal to the need. Most people who are in perfect health tell us they use 500 to 1000 milligrams of MPS per day. Those people with serious problems take 1200 to 3600 milligrams daily. You don't fight a forest fire with a garden hose. It is better to take more than less. I have never heard of a reaction from taking too much. I personally take about 3000 milligrams a day of an Aloe vera concentrate until I clear up a condition that I am concerned about. Then I reduce the intake somewhat, but continue taking the Aloe on a daily basis.

QUESTION
Which is better, concentrate or regular 1X Aloe?

ANSWER

If you have a quality brand of Aloe vera in the bottle, a 1X (single strength) is as good as a 15X (fifteen times stronger than 1X). The difference is that you need to take 15 times more of the 1X to achieve the same amount of the potentially beneficial active ingredients. One ounce of 15X is equal to 15 ounces of 1X

Cold processed concentrate has had percentages of the water removed via a single stage evaporator, resulting in less bulk, making it easier to store and more convenient for travel.

Aloe is not known for its taste, but you can mask the taste to suit your own taste-buds by adding the concentrate to your favorite beverage.

Concentrate costs less to ship because 1 bottle of 15X would equal 15 bottles of 1X.

QUESTION
Are all concentrates the same?

ANSWER
No. Many concentrates have had heat applied

as part of their process. One company, whose product we recently tested, processes their Aloe using a high heat evaporation and stabilization process which carmelizes the sugars and also breaks down the large chains which science believes contribute so valuably to healing. It also had extremely high levels of Aloin. Many companies are labeling their products concentrate when, in fact, testing reveals very little of the active ingredients in their products. In other words, their labels are misleading in that the amount of concentrate stated is grossly inaccurate.

QUESTION
Are the freeze-dried capsules as effective as the Aloe vera concentrate?

ANSWER
According to the people that are using both the capsules and liquid, they are achieving the same results.

QUESTION
I am a diabetic. Can I take Aloe?

ANSWER
Based on testimony and research, it would
appear that you can. You should monitor your
blood sugar level very closely, especially if you
are taking insulin. In every instance that I know
of, the diabetic's need of insulin was either
reduced or totally eliminated when they added
Aloe vera in sufficient quantities to their daily
diet.

QUESTION
Can I take Aloe along with other vitamins,
medicines and supplements?

ANSWER
Yes. As a matter of fact, most people report
back that their other products work better when
taken with Aloe.

QUESTION
I am really upset as I hear and read about the
frauds in the Aloe vera industry. What can I
do?

ANSWER
There are several things you can do. First,
refuse to buy Aloe vera products that haven't

been tested by an independent laboratory for sufficient Aloe content. Insist that the producer of the product furnish you with a copy of the independent testing results. If they won't supply the results, don't buy it. Second, educate your local health food stores and request that they carry only the best, tested Aloe vera products. And third, inform your friends and associates about the problem in the industry and tell them how they can determine what products are good.

QUESTION
What changes will I notice when taking Aloe vera for health maintenance rather than to treat a particular illness?

ANSWER
I cannot identify a specific change that you will notice. If you are rundown you will probably notice more dramatic changes than if you are in good health. I take the product daily because I know that it helps maintain my healthy condition. I do know that, since taking Aloe, I have developed greater resistance to illnesses such as the common cold, sore throats, and the flu. Also, my energy level is higher.

QUESTION

Why does the color and taste of Aloe vera vary so greatly?

ANSWER

That is a good, observant question and one of the most frequently asked questions. If you harvest the leaves after a long, dry period (no rain), it will reflect both a darker color and a much stronger taste. It also varies from season to season (summer vs. winter) therefore, variation in color and taste is very normal and should be expected.

QUESTION

Can I beneficially take Aloe directly from the Aloe vera plant?

ANSWER

Of course, but there are some things you need to be aware of. Both the inner and the outer skin have many of the important ingredients in them, but just under the skin is a yellowish substance called aloin. This substance is a very strong laxative. It should be removed and is in almost all Aloe vera products you purchase. If you take it from the plant, you should only use the centermost part of the leaf, the clear gel.

The plant loses most of its active, beneficial ingredients during its flowering period and should not be used at that time.

Make certain that the Aloe is freshly cut and used immediately. Without processing and preservatives, Aloe rapidly loses important properties. Finally, make certain that you really have an Aloe vera plant. Some plants are very similar but have few if any beneficial properties. There are over 200 species of Aloe vera. You should use the Barbadensis Miller plant.

Really, in almost all instances, it's easier to purchase a commercially prepared whole leaf Aloe vera concentrate that has been cold processed and tested for its MPS content.

QUESTION
How can I determine what is a good brand of Aloe vera to purchase?

ANSWER
There are several ways. First, look at the chart

I've prepared in Chapter 7 of this book, *Watch Out For The Frauds*. As I've said many times in my lecturers, "It doesn't take a nuclear scientist to see which brands are best."

Another way is to ask the experts. My company is always available to supply you with updated information. A third way is to ask people who have had success with Aloe vera what brands they use. Finally, you can have the product tested. I'll say more about this in the answer to the next question.

QUESTION
Can I do my own testing?

ANSWER
Yes, you can. We even sell an inexpensive test kit with simple instructions to follow. But beware. Some fraudulent companies are becoming more sophisticated. They are adding cheap ingredients which are of no medical value but which fool the simple tests. The more complex tests which can detect these additions as well as determine the presence and quantities of Aloe are expensive, usually running between $700 and $1,000 per test.

QUESTION
Why doesn't the government approve the use of Aloe vera as a drug?

ANSWER
They would, but to get registered as a drug would take several years and the cost would be between 100 and 150 million dollars. When registration is granted, the research company that spent all the money would not have any proprietary interest since Aloe vera is protected from patent.

QUESTION
Why doesn't the FDA stop those in the Aloe vera industry who are misrepresenting their product?

ANSWER
As I explained in Chapter 7, *Watch Out For The Frauds*, they have taken the ridiculous position that they cannot govern how much water is in Aloe vera. This position, of course, allows the unscrupulous to dilute the Aloe as much as they want. There is no labeling requirement to list how much water and how much Aloe is in a beverage.

QUESTION
Why didn't Aloe vera help my condition?

ANSWER
I don't know. But I will tell you this, in almost every case where a person has told me that they have received no benefit and I have been able to determine the brand of Aloe vera they used, it has been my opinion that the brand contained too small a quantity of Aloe in proportion to the amount of the product consumed to be of any benefit. Then you must be consistent and take the product every day. Also, Aloe is not a drug. It is a natural modality that helps supply you with your daily nutritional needs to keep your body defensive and able to fight against the invasion of disease or to rid your body of a disease already present. Aloe doesn't heal. Your body heals itself if it has the right defense weapons. We believe Aloe is one of those weapons.

QUESTION
If you were asked the question, "What is the best brand of Aloe vera available today," what would be your reply?

ANSWER
Look at the chart in Chapter 7. It is pretty obvious which, based upon a combination of price and Aloe content, is the best. Also, make certain that it is a product that is cold processed and is a whole leaf concentrate. If you still are unsure call Triputic.

QUESTION
Why doesn't the Aloe vera industry police its own and get rid of the frauds?

ANSWER
Greed. Too many of the big producers are part of the fraud. The best policing is for consumers to refuse to buy from the frauds.

QUESTION
Can I raise my own Aloe vera?

ANSWER
You should be able to. However if you live in a cold climate where it freezes in the winter, the plant should be grown indoors. It is hardy and takes very little care. Don't overwater it. Give it some occasional plant food and lots of sun.

QUESTION
How can I tell if a topical lotion or ointment has enough Aloe vera in it to be of any benefit?

ANSWER
Look at the label. The contents should be listed in percentage of volume. In most lotions and ointments Aloe is listed last or very near the end of ingredients. This tells you that the product has very little Aloe in it and in my opinion is of little or no worth. Aloe should be listed as the first ingredient on the label if you want to receive the maximum healing, soothing and skin care benefits from Aloe. One word of caution— buy from a reputable supplier of products. There are some dishonest ones in the industry that list Aloe not in the order of its percentage of volume.

QUESTION
One supplier indicates that only their Aloe product contains acemannan. Is this true.

ANSWER
All Aloe vera has acemannan in it. Acemannan comes from Aloe vera. The U.S. Adopted Names Council assigned the generic name

acemannan to a long chain sugar linked, acetylated polymannose found in Aloe vera and first
identified by Dr. Bill McAnalley.

QUESTION
What effect does using heat in treating Aloe vera
have?

ANSWER
Heat can carmelize the sugars and break down
the large saccharide chains which science believes contribute so valuably to healing.

QUESTION
Is Aloe vera a drug?

ANSWER
No. It is no more a drug than carrots or pota-
toes or peaches. It is a natural food. But just
as science is beginning to recognized the value
of grains, vegetables and fruits to our health, so
Aloe vera contributes to health as it strengthens
our immune systems.

QUESTION

So what then do you feel is Aloe vera's greatest contribution to good health and is it a panacea for all disease?

ANSWER
Probably the best way to answer this is to quote what Dr. Terry Pulse said, "If you can hold the progress of disease in check and if you can stimulate and enhance one's own defense mechanism, which is your immune system, there are no diseases that your own body is not capable of conquering and Aloe vera meets those principles."[61]

No, I would not go so far as to say that it is a panacea, but Aloe has been around for 4000 years and has obviously had great benefits to the body, more so than any other substance that we have discovered.

CHAPTER 11

SUMMING UP

Why, if any of you young gentlemen have a mind to get heard a mile off, you must make a bonfire of your reputation, and a close enemy of most men who wish you well.
John Jay Chapman[62]

You've reached the end of my story with Aloe vera. Really, though, I think it is only a beginning. I've told the story the way I see it, the way I believe it, and the way God gave it to me. There are those in the Aloe vera industry who will be angry with some things I revealed. That's all right. My loyalty is to you, the reader, to my conscience, and to my God, not to them.

With time there will be many more miraculous healing stories to report and scientific studies to disclose. And we'll learn more about how the components in Aloe work in and on our bodies.

Years ago a brilliant professor related the fictional story of a man who claimed that he had found a beautiful, uncut diamond in his backyard. I have changed the facts somewhat. The historians discounted the story because no other diamonds had been found in the area throughout history. The geologists cried impossible because it wasn't the right type of strata in which to find diamonds. The psychologists noted the wording the discoverer used in describing what he had found. It was similar they said to the wording that known pathological liars had used. The sociologists took a poll. The majority of those responding did not believe that the diamond was real and so the sociologists concluded similarly. The scientists snubbed the discovery. There were no controlled studies on diamonds being found in backyards. So the historians, the geologists, the psychologists, the sociologists, and the scientists all decided that the diamond was a fake. Finally someone said, "Why not test the diamond?" And they did. It was genuine.

The story is so analogous to Aloe vera and its critics. To all I would say, "Don't believe me. Don't believe the testimonies of others. Don't believe the available scientific studies. Just try it and then draw your own conclusion."

I close with my own testimony. In October of 1988, my appendix ruptured. While in surgery, they discovered a tumor the size of a 100 watt light bulb on my transverse colon and three growths on the inside of the colon. My colon was also covered with diverticulitis. They had to remove the growths inside the colon with laser surgery, rectally. At this time, they found two small tumors on my prostate. They told my wife that within one year, if my colon continued to deteriorate, a colostomy would be necessary. This meant removing the colon and carrying a bag on my side. I got serious about taking Aloe vera and I drank about four ounces per day of the whole leaf Aloe vera concentrate. I have had follow-up physical exams annually and my prostate and PSA counts are both within normal ranges. I have had no other problems with my colon, whatsoever. I was also on a high blood-pressure medication which I have since discontinued and my blood pressure is within normal ranges. My cholesterol count was very elevated and is now in the low, normal range. Aloe vera did it.

I have found my mission.

BI-MONTHLY UPDATE

Doctor Lee Ritter and his company Triputic, provide a news report every other month. *TRIPUTIC, Nature's Healing and Health Update.*

As well as providing new information on Aloe Vera, the report keeps the reader abreast of the newest discoveries in medical and health treatment, successful health programs, medicines, and natural supplements.

Included are articles from experts in the field of health, nutrition, medicine, and law. A consumer report evaluates available health products and treatments. As one recent reader commented, *The news report is superb. No health conscious person can afford to be without it.*

Triputic
P.O. Box 116307
Carrollton, Texas
1-800-331-1678

NOTES AND REFERENCES

Chapter One. "My Mission Unfolds"

1. Santayana, G. (1980). O world, thou choosest not. *In Bartlett's Familiar Quotations* (15th ed.) (p. 703). Boston: Toronto, London: Little Brown and Company.

2. Pulse, T. L., Uhlig, E., Rueckert, P., & English, C. (1989). *A significant improvement in a clinical pilot study utilizing nutritional supplements, essential fatty acids and stabilized Aloe vera juice in 29 HIV seropositive, ARC and AIDS patients.* Grand Prairie, TX: Terry L. Pulse, pp. 3-4.

Chapter Two. "Seeing Is Believing"

3. Meridith, G. (1980). The egoist. In *Bartlett's*, p.600.

Chapter Three. "Aloe Vera's 4000 Year Old History."

4. New York Trust Co, v. Eisner, (1921) 256 U.S. 345, 349.

5. Coats, B. C. (1984). *The Silent Healer, a modern study of Aloe Vera.* Bill C. Coats, p.11.

6. Kent, C. M. (1979). *Aloe Vera*. Arlington, VA: Carol Miller Kent, p. 5.

7. Coats, p. 11.

8.   Skousen, M. B. (undated). *The Aloe Vera handbook.* Garden Grove, CA: Max B. Skousen, p.4.

9.   Agarwal, O.P. (1985). Prevention of atheromatousheart disease. *Angiology, the Journal of Vascular Disease*, p. 485.

10.   Agarwal, p. 485.

11.   Agarwal, pp. 485-490.

12.   Kent, p. 20.

13.   Dioscordes. (undated) The Greek herbal of Dioscordes. In *Aloe Vera, quotations from medical journals.* Garden Grove, CA: Max B. Skousen, pp. 125-126.

14.   Hennessee, O. M. and Cook, B. R. (1989). *Aloe, myth-magic medicine.* Lawton, OK: Universal Graphics, p.11.

15.   Dr. Madis Laboratories. Veragel, purified Aloe leaf extract derived from Aloe vera gel. In *Quotations from medical journals on Aloe research.* Cypress, CA: Aloe Vera Research Institute, p. 1.

16.   Madis Laboratories, p.2.

17.   Madis Laboratories, p.2

Chapter Four. "Testimonies"

18. Isaiah 8:20. *The Bible.*

19. Sheets, M. A., Unger, B. A., Giggleman, G. F. Jr., & Tizard, I. R. (1991). Studies of the effect of acemannan on retrovirus infections: clinical stabilization of feline leukemia virus-infected cats. *Mol. Biother.* 3 (Mar), pp.41-45.

20. Sheets, pp. 43-44.

21. McPherson, J. (1993). Letter to Lee Ritter. In possession of Lee Ritter.

22. Lightinheart, J (1993). Oral account to Lee Ritter. Transcript possession of Lee Ritter.

23. Pulse, T. L., (1989) *Aloe Vera, Nature's Miracle.* (Video Cassette Recording). Aurora, CO: Lee Ritter.

24. Henson, M. K. (1993). Letter to Lee Ritter. In possession of Lee Ritter.

25. McKittrick, L. (1992). Letter to Lee Ritter. In possession of Lee Ritter.

26. Kohn, R. A. (undated) Letter to Lee Ritter. In possession of Lee Ritter.

27. Yannacito, A. (1992). Letter to Lee Ritter. In possession of Lee Ritter.

28.   Arrington, M. (1989). *Aloe Vera, Nature's Miracle.* (Video Cassette Recording).

29.   Cooper, S. S. (1992). Letter to Lee Ritter. In posses-- sion of Lee Ritter.

30.   Knox, J. H. (1992). Letter to Lee Ritter. In possession of Lee Ritter.

31.   Unidentified. (1992) Oral account to Lee Ritter.

32.   Hart, K. *The Valley Herald.* Dec 23, 1987., p.3.

33.   Harrison, J. (1992). Aloe in dentistry. *Health Consciousness.* 13 (1) p.20.

34.   Ritter, S. (1992). Statement in possession of Lee Ritter.

35.   Boyles, J. E. (1992). Letter to Dr. Roy Kupinsel, M.D. Copy in possession of Lee Ritter.

36.   Younglund, J. (1992). Letter to Lee Ritter. In posses- sion of Lee Ritter.

37.   Wood, J. M. (1993). Oral account to Lee Ritter. Transcript in possession of Lee Ritter.

38.   Oliver, H. G. (1993). Letter to Lee Ritter. In posses- sion of Lee Ritter.

39.   Shawchuck, N. (1993). Letter to Lee Ritter. In posses- sion of Lee Ritter.

40. Younglund.

Chapter Five. "Science Investigates"

41. McDaniel, H. R. (1989). *Aloe Vera, Nature's Miracle.* (Video Cassette Recording)

42. Agarwal, pp. 485-490.

43. Agarwal, p. 490.

44. Pulse, pp. 22-23.

45. Sheets, pp.41-45.

46. Sheets, p.43.

Chapter Six. "How Aloe Vera Works"

47. Johnson, S. (1980). Life of Johnson. In *Bartlett's,* p.355.

48. Ray Dirks Research. (1992). The acemannan report. *Health Consciousness* 13 (1)., pp. 43-46.

49. Heinerman, J. (1982). *Aloe Vera, JoJoba and Yucca.* New Canaan, CN: Keats Publishing, Inc., p.5.

Chapter Seven. "Watch Out For The Frauds"

50. Tennyson, A. L. (1980). The grandmother. In *Bartlett's*, p.535.

51.   Danhof, I. E., (1991). North Texas Research Laboratory. Lab report dated 29 Mar 1991. Report in possession of Lee Ritter.

52.   McDaniel.

Chapter Eight. "About AIDS"

53.   Pulse, *Aloe Vera, Nature's Miracle.* (Video Cassette Recording)

54.   Strecker, R. B., (1988). *The Strecker Memorandum.* (Video Cassette Recording) Eagle Rock, CA: The Strecker Group.

Chapter Nine. "What You Should Know About The Food And Drug Administration"

55.   De Balzac, H. (1992). Bureaucracy, the works of Honore de Balzac. In *Respectfully Quoted, a Dictionary of Quotations from the Library of Congress.* Washington, D.C.: Congressional Quarterly Inc., p.139.

56.   New York Times News Service. Acne drug causing birth flaws.

57.   Douglass, W. C. (1990). The AZT scandal. *The Cutting Edge.* 4 (12) Dec. 1990, pp. 2-6.

58.   Douglass, p. 6.

59.   Sawaya, Z. (1991). Getting even. *Forbes* 29 Apr 1991,
       pp. 94-95.

60.   Samuel, P. (1992) Who will regulate the regulators?
       National Review. 2 Nov 1992, pp. 38-39.

61.   McDaniel.

Chapter Eleven. "Summing Up"

62.   Chapman, J. J. (1910). *The Unity of Human Nature.*
       Learning and Other Essays. (reprinted 1961). Geneva,
       NY: Hobart Chapter of Phi Beta Kappa, Hobart College,
       p.185.

APPENDIX

PRODUCT	TEST DATE	BATCH	MPS/LITER	SIZE
TRIPUTIC			Page 1	
ALOE TEST RESULTS				
Aloe Ace	10-92	-------	13,610	4 oz
Aloe Ace	04-92	-------	7,840	4 oz
Aloe Complete	07-93	127	8,490	Liter
Aloe Farms	01-93	1181	570	32 oz
Aloe Int'l.	03-91	32857	160	Liter
Aloe Master 1X	08-93	2669	3,840	Liter
Aloe Master 10X	02-96	B2101G	17,000	32 oz
Aloe Master 10X	04-95	1402	18,054	32 oz
Aloe Master 10X	03-94	031594	16,600	32 oz
Aloe Master 10X	02-94	013094	16,360	32 oz
Aloe Master 10X	05-93	3535A	17,750	32 oz
Aloe Master 15X	04-95	E1002F	21,304	16 oz
Aloe Master 15X	07-93	B266B	19,010	16 oz
Aloe Plus	03-91	9722G	610	32 oz
Coats Aloe Int'l.	09-91	2208	2,200	32 oz
Cytoplan	02-96	B0601	17,000	Drum
Deveras- Carrington	04-91	101161	1,640	Liter
Diamite-Vitality	04-92	11136	1,960	Liter
Forever Living	10-92	NB28	1,960	Liter
Fultonia Health Inst.	07-93	C3532	13,590	Liter
George's	03-91	3632	0	Gal
George's	05-92	4123	0	Gal

	Triputic			Page 2
	ALOE TEST RESULTS			
PRODUCT	TEST DATE	BATCH	MPS/LITER	SIZE
Jason Winter's Finest	10-92	------	590	32 oz
Kaire Int'l.	03-96	C0501G	10,000+	Liter
Lametco	12-92	1113	10,200	Liter
Lametco	12-91	111591	7,840	Liter
Multiway Aloe Gel	10-92	21351	1,230	Gal
Natural High Aloe	10-92	------	40	16 oz
Nature's Nutri. Aloe plus	05-94	43034	280	16 oz
Nature's Sunshine	10-92	190828	290	32 oz
Oriana True Aloe	02-92	------	3,390	Liter
R Pur Aloe 15 X	10-91	263	8,860	16 oz
R Pur Aloe 15 X	11-91	2665	2,280	16 oz
R Pur Aloe 15 X	10-94	C4307	9,260	16 oz
Rio Grande Aloe	07-93	1463	120	32 oz
Aloe Maia- Sterling Health	04-95	4340301	17,916	32 oz
Sunrider	02-93	812552	60	32 oz

Flavored Drinks with Aloe Fillet: These Aloe Drinks have a new unique process that is high in MPS count and also contain natural herbal combinations that is believed to benefits the immune system. These products are not concentrates. We at Triputic highly endorse and recommend these companies products. Use for daily body maintenance. Contains from 1000 to 3000 MPS/Liter. Suggest 8 to 16 oz a day. Children love these drinks.

AMI   Oxyfresh   Team up   Shaperite   Trader Joe's

DEPARTMENT OF HEALTH & HUMAN SERVICES   Public Health Service

==
                                         Food and Drug Administration
                                         Building 20-Denver Federal Center
                                         Post Office Box 25087
                                         Denver, Colorado 80225-0087
                                         303-236-3000 (FTS: 776-3000)

February 15, 1991

CERTIFIED MAIL
RETURN RECEIPT REQUESTED

Mr. Leland A. Ritter
CEO
Triputic, Inc.
11912 North Washington
Northglenn, CO 80233

                          REGULATORY LETTER

Dear Mr. Ritter:

This letter is written in reference to the marketing of various products by your
firm containing aloe vera, including Aloe Rich Concentrated Aloe Vera, Aloe
Pearl, Garolic, Klean and Klear, Aloe Rich True Soap, Aloe Creme and Liniment.
Promotional material (labeling) including but not necessarily limited to your
pamphlets "A to Z Why Aloe Vera Works," "Aloe Myth-Magic Medicines," "Nature's
Miracle Aloe Vera Miracle Healing Plant;" the letter dated October 24, 1990, to
Triputic, Inc. from Dr. Terry L. Pulse, M.D.; the letter dated June 16, 1990, to
Mr. Lee Ritter from Wertz and Associates; the abstract concerning AIDS research
done by Dr. Terry L. Pulse, M.D.; and the video tape "Nature's Miracle", which
are distributed with your products, state or suggest that these products are
useful in treating or preventing a variety of diseases, including AIDS,
diabetes, high blood pressure, multiple sclerosis, karposis sarcoma - skin
cancer, malignancies, and many other diseases.

Because such labeling includes statements which represent and suggest that the
articles are intended to be used in the cure, mitigation, treatment, or
prevention of disease, or are intended to affect the structure or any function
of the body of man, these products are drugs within the meaning of section
201(g) of the Federal Food, Drug, and Cosmetic Act (the Act). Further, we are
unaware of any substantial scientific evidence which documents that these drugs
are generally recognized as safe and effective for the above referenced disease
conditions or any other disease conditions.

Triputic, Inc.
February 15, 1991
Page 2

Accordingly, marketing of these drugs is a violation of the Act, as follows:

Section	Brief Description

502(a)
: The aforesaid articles of drug are misbranded in that their labeling is false and misleading by representations and suggestions that there is substantial scientific evidence to establish that the articles are safe and effective for use in the treatment of various diseases.

502(f)(1)
: The articles of drug are misbranded in that their labeling fails to bear adequate directions for use in the treatment of the various diseases referenced in their promotional material. They are not exempt from this requirement under regulation 21 CFR 201.115 since the articles are new drugs within the meaning of section 201(p) and no approval of any application filed pursuant to section 505(b) is effective for these drugs.

The articles of drug are further misbranded in that their labeling does not contain adequate directions for use as this term is defined in 21 CFR 201.5 since the conditions for which they are offered are not amendable to self diagnosis and treatment by the laity; therefore, adequate directions for use cannot be written under which the layman can use these drugs safely and for the purposes for which they are intended.

505(a)
: The aforesaid articles are drugs within the meaning of Section 201(g) of the Act which may not be introduced or delivered for introduction into interstate commerce under section 505(a) of the Act, since they are new drugs within the meaning of section 201(p) of the Act and no approval of any application filed pursuant to section 505(b) is effective for such drugs.

Subsequent to our December 12, 1990. inspection of your firm, our office received several documents from you concerning the Ninth Amendment to the United States Constitution. You should be aware that it is incumbent upon you as the most responsible corporate officer to assure that all products which your firm distributes are in compliance with all provisions of the Act.

Triputic, Inc.
February 15, 1991
Page 3

We request that you reply within ten (10) days of your receipt of this letter
stating the action you will take to discontinue the marketing of these drug
products. If such corrective action is not promptly undertaken, the Food and
Drug Administration is prepared to initiate legal action to enforce the law.
The Act provides for seizure of illegal products, and/or injunction against
the manufacturer and distributor of illegal products (21 U.S.C. 332 and 334).
Your response should be directed to Shelly L. Maifarth, Compliance Officer, at
the above address.

Sincerely,

James F. Yoger
Acting District Director

DEPARTMENT OF HEALTH & HUMAN SERVICES Public Health Service

===

            Food and Drug Administration
            Building 20-Denver Federal Center
            P.O. Box 25087
            Denver, Colorado 80225-0087
            303-236-3000 (FTS: 776-3000)

May 16, 1991

Mr. Leland A. Ritter
CEO
Triputic, Inc.
11912 North Washington
Northglenn, Colorado 80233

Dear Mr. Ritter:

Enclosed you will find the literature which you submitted in March, 1991 for
Shelly Maifarth to review. Our office has neither the time nor the resources
available to review this material. If you have any specific questions this
office will be happy to assist you. For your information, I have enclosed a
copy of the Federal Food, Drug, and Cosmetic Act with the appropriate sections
highlighted regarding the definitions of "drugs" and "food".

       Sincerely,

       Regina A. Barrell
       Acting Compliance Officer